Even As I Am

NEAL A. MAXWELL

Deseret Book Company
Salt Lake City, Utah

First printing in paperbound edition, March 1991

ISBN 0-87747-943-7 (hardbound ed.)
ISBN 0-87579-614-1 (paperbound ed.)

Printed in the United States of America
10   9   8   7   6   5   4   3   2   1

To Harold B. Lee, eleventh President and Prophet of The Church of Jesus Christ of Latter-day Saints in this dispensation—a seer and a special witness of Jesus Christ—with appreciation for his tutoring friendship and with anticipation of reunion and resumption. The cessation of his leadership here was a glorious inauguration there among those whom, as especially foretold, he continues his special labors.

Contents

Preface

Appreciation is gladly given for Elder James E. Talmage's work *Jesus the Christ,* from which I first benefited as a young missionary, but also ever since. Gratitude is also due to President J. Reuben Clark, Jr., for the painstaking way in which he converged the chronology and concepts of Jesus' ministry and teachings in his publication *Our Lord of the Gospels.* More recently, I have been blessed, as have many others, by the multiple and scripture-enriched volumes of my colleague, Elder Bruce R. McConkie, about the Messiah. Each of these works stands on its merits, reflecting the message, talents, and emphasis of the authors.

This volume seeks to bear my own witness and to give my own emphasis and testimony of Jesus Christ. (Rev. 1:2; D&C 76:82.) If there are any incorrect thoughts or words in this volume, that detract from His words, may these be allowed to "fall to the ground" unheeded. (See 1 Sam. 3:19; 2 Kgs. 10:10; Alma 37:17; D&C 1:38.)

Use will be made of selected events and incidents for the purpose of discussing not only Jesus' *actuality,* but also

His remarkable *personality* and His unparalleled development of the eternal attributes of the Father. These episodes
will, of course, underscore His divinity, but they will also
tell us much that we need to know about the personality of
Jesus, since we have been told clearly that we are to strive
to become as He is.

We will examine Jesus' tutoring relationship with His
followers in the traditional framework, such as those involving Moses, Peter, and Paul, but also with other
prophets, such as Enoch, Moroni, and Joseph Smith. We
obviously learn more of Him by studying the *fullness* of His
ministry. Studying the Savior's life at any one point provides single episodes that stir us and deservedly claim our
attention. But it is the accumulation of episodes that produces awe and adoration of Him—all the more reason to
ponder the fullness of His ministry.

As we examine "this Jesus Christ" (3 Ne. 11:2), most of
our information about His life comes through the four Gospels of the New Testament. These priceless texts chronicle
that portion of His existence wherein the Savior of all mankind was, so to speak, "in residence." Prior and later, He
made important visitations elsewhere, giving corroborat-
ing testimony and making additional declarations, such as
to His "other sheep," as in the Americas, and, sub-
sequently, to the so-called lost tribes. (See 3 Ne. 15:17, 21.)
In these and other visits, He repeated many of His basic
teachings and sermons; He also provided additional vital
instructions and certain amplifications.

However, there was only one birth at Bethlehem, one
period when He was a carpenter's son, one Gethsemane,
one Judas Iscariot, and one Calvary. Praise be to those who
preserved those precious and singular episodes in our
Holy Bible!

We do not, by any means, have all that Jesus said. Some of His teachings to His closest disciples have not been shared with others, and for very appropriate reasons. (John 21:25; 3 Ne. 26:6.)

Furthermore, even where we do have His words, we learn of His facial expressions and accompanying gestures only rarely. For example, we do read about Him when He was angry (Matt. 21:12; Mark 3:5), and when He wept (John 11:35; 3 Ne. 17:21-22). We learn of the look He gave to Peter (Luke 22:61), and how He smiled upon His praying apostles and disciples (3 Ne. 19:25, 30).

Jesus clearly had the unique capacity of being able to respond truthfully to inquiries and circumstances in a manner that addressed the immediate audience as well as the needs of eventual audiences. On occasion, He said things that might have seemed stern, even harsh, at the moment in order to teach an eternal truth.

How His glorious words have held up under the scrutiny of the centuries! Though His teachings are deep in the demands made upon us, He has taught us also by explanation and example how to "be of good cheer" as we pass through the proving and tutoring process of mortality.

Acknowledgment is gladly given, therefore, to all who over the centuries have written and preserved the precious and illuminating words about our "precious Savior, dear Redeemer."

Acknowledgments

More than the usual gratitude is expressed to those who assisted with this book. Given its special focus on Jesus Christ, the rigors of writing were matched by the need for candid and thoughtful review by friends—Jeffrey R. Holland, Elizabeth Haglund, Roy W. Doxey, and Lowell M. Durham, Jr.—who did not disappoint. As busy and able as these friends are in their own realms, they took time to respond to an early draft and to suggest improvements that clearly affected the subsequent structure of this volume.

From another friend, Robert H. Garff, came encouragement to elaborate on the author's tribute to Jesus Christ in the October 1981 general conference of the Church.

Careful and patient editorial review has been performed by Eleanor Knowles. And perhaps the most patience of all came from Jeananne Hornbarger in the typing of the various drafts. She, too, urged me on in moments of busyness and weariness when the project might have been set aside.

As always, my wife, Colleen, was ever encouraging—but also reminding of what the focus should be, and also of the need for the book to be specifically helpful to the readers in their efforts to live as Jesus lived.

Even with the deep appreciation for the help of all the above, what is said is my responsibility and mine alone. The failures and shortcomings are clearly mine, while any real value which might appear in these pages is attributable to a Special Friend.

1

Eternal Purpose in Christ Jesus

In a setting of irreligion or vague religion, both of which abound in our contemporary culture, not only to certify Jesus' *actuality* but also to write of His *personality* constitutes marked counterpoint.

In a permissive society that is increasingly unconcerned with virtue, it is even more unusual to testify in apostolic affirmation of the clear requirement that the Father and Jesus have undeniably laid upon us mortals: to strive, individually, to become like them.

In the scriptures, however, we encounter truths and requirements that are at the center of personal, global, and "eternal purpose . . . in Christ Jesus."[1] Therefore, this deliberate, divine seriousness underlies not only our need to worship God, but also to know *what* we worship. Jesus declared this in a telling conversation with a woman of Samaria: "Ye worship ye know not what: we know what we worship."[2]

Much of the message of the holy scriptures concerns the

1

nature, character, and attributes of God and His Son, Jesus Christ: "I give unto you these sayings that you may understand and know how to worship, and know what you worship, that you may come unto the Father in my name, and in due time receive of his fulness."[3]

Therefore, it becomes clear both logically and scripturally that the only real *veneration* of Jesus is *emulation* of Him. Indeed, striving to become like Him is a special way of bearing and sharing our testimony of Him.

Jesus has told us that if we truly love Him, we will keep His commandments; and keeping and doing His commandments surely puts and keeps us on the lengthy pathway to perfection.

None of the divine data given to us about the Father and the Son are provided merely to give us an interesting theological backdrop for our mortal musings. The revelation of Jesus Christ is so much more relevant and demanding of us than that, as these next interactive verses make soberingly and abundantly clear:

"*Be ye therefore perfect*, even as your Father which is in heaven is perfect."

"Ye are therefore commanded to be perfect, even as your Father who is in heaven is perfect."

"Therefore I would that ye should be perfect even as I, or your Father who is in heaven is perfect."

"Therefore, what manner of men ought ye to be? Verily I say unto you, *even as I am*."[4]

The Greek rendering of the word *perfect* is *finished, complete, fully developed*—but whichever the synonym, it is an awesome requirement. Yet it *is* a requirement. Striving for this excellence is not an elective. No wonder Paul wrote of the "eternal purpose" that the Father "purposed in Christ Jesus our Lord."[5] And no wonder that the Prophet Joseph

Smith taught that "a correct idea of [God's] character, perfections, and attributes" is necessary to the development and exercise of true faith in God.[6]

Vagueness about the true nature of God—"what" we worship—has taken a terrible toll in the world. Such vagueness subtly feeds faithlessness and adds to the sense of purposelessness that needlessly permeates so many lives. Someday we shall see how much boredom and drift (as well as both dread and disdain of death) are rooted in the incorrect and inadequate perceptions of God. Those in ancient Israel were not alone in following false gods "to [their] hurt."[7]

Besides, the teachings of Jesus Christ have never been rejected because His standards are imprecise or insufficiently high. His teachings have, in fact, been disregarded by some because they are viewed as being too precise and impractically high! Yet such lofty standards, when followed, produce the truest and highest happiness. There is no other individual to compare with Jesus Christ, nor any other message to rival that of Jesus—a message that is so holistic, so consistent, and so explanatory of what we earthlings are experiencing in mortality.[8]

Passive acknowledgment of an aimless and diluted deity does little to improve the human condition. And militant followership of tribal deity who issues no equivalent of the second commandment is dangerous. But sincere followership of the living God—who urges us to be like Him in love, justice, kindness, mercy, and purity—can redeem both the individual and mankind. Understanding what we worship is, thus, no trivial theological point—it is purpose itself!

Discovering and pursuing such eternal purpose is made no easier as the second coming of our Lord draws ever nearer and the prophesied conditions appear, such as the foreseen perplexity among nations and uncertainty of our war-filled times. Appearing, too, is the foreseen ambivalence toward the divinity of the Savior—even by many so-called Christians and, ironically, some clerics. An earlier apostle, Peter, foretold how, in the last days, some would even deny the divinity of Jesus, who purchased humanity—and at such a price.[9] When else in human history have the ransomed complained about the ransomer or ignored their benefactor?

Yet while we live in an age in which many hold religion in disdain, so many other people openly hunger, soulfully and deeply, for an understanding of how things really are and really will be, for purposes that outlast the moment. They are kept from the truth only because they "know not where to find it."[10] This search for meaning is the search for an explanation of self and of life, and for the underlying purposes of the universe. This deep craving for truth is expressed in many ways by many mortals, often directly, other times indirectly; sometimes foolishly, other times wisely. Blessed are those who have found *the* truth and have, thereby, been made free, and who have learned that there is both eternal and personal purpose!

It is the beginning of wisdom for us mortals to accept the simple but verifiable truths about eternal purpose as found in Jesus Christ. He has summed it all up, commencing with the words "This is my gospel."[11] The straightforward explanation that follows each of these declarations gives to mankind the "good news"—the glorious news—concerning Jesus' coming as our Rescuer and our Savior and our Atoner. His gospel gives to humankind the answers to the search for meaning and eternal purpose.

Regarding eternal purpose, the words in this book are

designed to help us to "be of good cheer," lest we be numbered among those whose hearts fail them in the last days.[12] Some of the current causes for despair and discouragement should be no mystery: skepticism about the historicity of Jesus; the mistaken view that a value-free society is free; schools that lack moral content; family Bibles that go unread; and fewer and fewer families that are intact and nourishing, and so forth. Alas, when the hopes of humans are riddled and blasted, it is usually when mortals assume that familiar formation: the circular firing squad.

Unsurprisingly, this decline in true religion has occurred at the same time as the rise in behavioral permissiveness. Such permissiveness has not been generated solely by the people; often it has been promoted by those who pretend to be religious leaders but who are consumed with other causes. To them, our crucial task of developing the divine attributes is regarded as out of reach or as a diversion.[13] Why be concerned with developing one's mercy when there is a corrupt government to be toppled? Why worry over containing sexual hunger within the bounds of chastity and fidelity when there is so much other hunger in the world?

The consequences of such attitudes and conditions are felt—inevitably, diversely, but irrevocably. Yet the plans of God are not set aside merely because some humans have tried to set Him aside or because some deny the divinity of His Son, Jesus Christ.

Happily, modern revelation not only affirms the reality of the existence and lordship of Jesus Christ, of whom the prophets have spoken, but it also provides us with this needed affirmation in a time of increasing despair and increasing doubt. In ways yet unclear, we shall even see how the Book of Mormon, "these last records," "shall establish the truth of the first" records, the Holy Bible.[14] And the central truth to be established by both interactive books of scripture is the glorious fact that the Lamb of God is the Son of the Eternal Father, and the Savior of the world whose pattern provides for us purpose for mortality and whose atonement gives us the inestimable blessings of immortality.

The various appearances of the resurrected Christ to over three thousand souls make it clear who He was and is. Additional scriptures attest to the reality of the resurrected Christ. Added to the traditional list of those who saw Him, such as Saul and Stephen, are names like Jacob, Nephi, Lamoni, Emer, Mormon, and Moroni. How fortunate that we are not left alone with the antiquity of previous testimonies and revelations, marvelous and needed as those are!

There is no need for doubt merely because of the passage of time. Growing historical distance from certain events need not pose a special problem for those in our day who desire to believe in and to behave in accordance with God's eternal purpose in Jesus Christ.

In the precious Acts of the Apostles, we read the declaration of how Jesus "shewed himself alive after his passion by many infallible proofs, being seen of them forty days, and speaking of the things pertaining to the kingdom of God."[15] These "infallible proofs" included, said Paul, the multiple appearances of Jesus that affirmed His resurrected status.

Infallible proofs of the same type and description have been amply provided in this dispensation, too.[16]

It is very important to understand how the events of the restoration reinforce these last-recited and fundamental realities about Jesus. Modern revelation dissolves the doubts and distortions about His divinity. The restoration, therefore, not only constitutes a glorious *restitution*, but also a stern, head-on *refutation!*

So many implications, for instance, flow from the illuminating and confirming first vision granted to Joseph Smith as well as from subsequent appearances in our day of the Savior and His ancient prophets. For instance, since Jesus came to *restore* his Church, then it is clear that He established an authorized church while He was on earth before—contrary to what some maintain who believe that He gave some helpful ethical pronouncements in the meridian of time and merely let it go at that. Remember, had Jesus been of the world, the world would have loved Him![17]

Since Jesus came in the early part of the nineteenth century to select and call a new, youthful prophet, He continues to work through prophets, just as He did in the past. Moreover, He dispatched other great leaders, such as Moses, Elijah, Elias, John the Baptist, Peter, James, and John, to assist the new prophet in launching the last dispensation. Christ operates not only through an organized church, but also through priesthood keys of authority, circumspectly honoring those who held certain keys in previous dispensations.

Jesus' use of ancient American records in undergirding the restoration also signifies how important it is to have a second scriptural witness for Christ in the form of the Book of Mormon, to join the marvelous Holy Bible. Should it surprise us? Jesus, as Jehovah, in His justice, insisted on establishing facts in the mouths of two or three witnesses, and He would have it so in order to confirm His resurrection, the most important fact of all.[18]

Our faith can be freshened in yet other ways. Those fed at the miracle of the loaves and fishes have long since gone to their reward, as have also the ten lepers. However, the same Lord who fed and healed loves us no less, nor is He less powerful than He was two thousand years ago. How blessed we are to have "proofs" of the longevity of His Lordship! Moreover, His working out of the miracle of the Atonement gives us each everlasting blessings, while the wine produced in the miracle at Cana is long gone. Jesus' blessings, both personal and universal, continue with us to this very day. Little wonder, then, that the adversary sought to extinguish the tiny light of the Restoration before it could fully flame and reilluminate these great realities! It is not difficult either to see both why and how the adversary has feverishly worked to deflect people from carefully considering Jesus in His true role in carrying out the Father's eternal purposes.

Alas, however, some still settle for regarding Jesus as a mere figure in folklore. Others see Him as a significant moral, but nevertheless mortal, teacher—a Socrates of Samaria, a Plato of Palestine. Still others regard Him as the respected founder of a sect that became yet another widespread religious movement to take its place alongside several other large, worldwide religious movements. Many do accord Him a vague form of Lordship, mistakenly assuming, however, that though He lived and is risen, He has receded somewhere into distant space.[19]

But men are not mere ciphers in a vast but dumb space; they are everlasting and accountable individuals. Modern witnesses affirm the meaningfulness of life, human identity, human belonging. The vastness of God's creations are the *verification* of meaning, not its *annihilation*. There is eternal purpose, and it is to be found in the Father's Only Begotten, Christ Jesus.

Therefore, when we say "He lives," we mean all that that glorious truth implies. The theophany at Palmyra, for instance, was a deeply profound statement, not solely an affirmation to that youthful audience of one, *but to all mankind.* The chorus of resurrected notables who, representing ages past, later appeared to Joseph Smith, such as at the Kirtland Temple, gave to us an anthem of assurance.[20] And what is more, these great, ordering, and reassuring realities will not go away just because some reject them. After all, the Lord's plan of salvation is not a set of floor plans for a new house that we as clients can modify or reject. The Architect is not our employee, but our Host, even the Lord of Hosts; He is not only our Landlord, He is also our Lord!

Strangely, it is not only the fullness of the gospel that is rejected by some, but the fullness of its attending implications. Questions and reservations about Jesus' historicity may, for some, merely be a cover for a refusal to face not only His reality but also the realities and implications of His gospel truths. Some lives, alas, are far too entangled in the webbing of the world to make it easy to entertain the implications that radiate from the reality of the resurrected Jesus.

We are, nevertheless, at the center of God's eternal purposes, for He has told us what His work and His glory consist of.[21] There can be no sense of purpose—no lasting purpose—for us that exists apart from His purposes. And Christ Jesus is our Atoner and Advocate—our Rescuer and Exemplar. His gospel is *the* "good news." Yet it is the oldest news ever!

It is in this setting that a long-held desire to write a book about Jesus Christ in tribute to and testimony of Him comes to fruition. With the author's calling to the holy apostleship in the summer of 1981, the subsequent ordination thereto, and the conferring of the solemn duties that go with being a special witness of Jesus Christ and His name in all the world, this most demanding but most deserving task has been undertaken.

While the fundamental and summational content of the testimony of all the special witnesses in behalf of the Savior will be the same, the manner in which the witness is given and the emphasis within that witness will, of necessity, differ with the personalities of these men. Likewise, such witnessing seeks to respond to the existing circumstances of those to whom their witness is addressed.

Having gladly forgone what could have been a career in government and politics (the former constitute "the road not taken" for which there is *no* regret at all, since those chores are being better done by others anyway), I gladly give full attention to the task of being a special witness.

Once another and better church leader, Alma, determined to forgo his governmental chores in order to give full attention to his spiritual ministry. He chose to bear down in pure testimony and to stir his people up "in remembrance of their duty."[22] These pages seek to stir us in our duty to become like the Savior. The words to follow, however, represent not even "the smallest part which I feel"[23] by way of God's "eternal purpose . . . in Christ Jesus" and by way of sharing my testimony about the reality that Jesus lives—with all that that glorious fact implies.

More and more, whatever my tasks and activities of the moment, or my thought patterns, there stands the Savior—whether in needed remonstration or in needed inspiration. What *He* is presses in upon me in relentless reminder of what *I* should be. What He has generously given me elicits deep gratitude and deepens my trust. His impending blessings are a spur to me to intensify my discipleship.

I find I can do nothing *without Him*. Yet, alas, how often He can do so little *with me*. It is increasingly difficult for me to sing those hymns that pay special tribute to Him without becoming misty-eyed. Whether in the temple, on a high-way, or in a jet airplane, the reflections and reminders about Him come in waves, like refreshing yet subduing surf. And, on occasion, of a night, "I am full of tossings to and fro unto the dawning of the day."[24]

So it is that the time to try has come—the time to testify not only of Jesus' transcendent actuality, but also to His resplendent personality. Through examining and describing His matchless attributes in action, I find the conclusion is inescapable: how earnestly we are to strive to accept His generous but genuine invitation and direction to become, as He has said, "Even as I am."[25]

Footnotes

[1]Ephesians 3:11.

[2]John 4:22-26. "Samaritan worship was a strange intermixture of pagan and Israelite doctrine. Centuries before they had added the worship of Jehovah to the worship of their idols; now this higher form of worship had become the dominant force in their way of worship, and their rituals and performances were dominantly Mosaic in nature, but still their worship was both Jewish and pagan all wrapped in one." (Bruce R. McConkie, *The Mortal Messiah* 1 [Deseret Book, 1979]: 499.)

[3]D&C 93:19.

[4]Matthew 5:48; JST Matthew 5:50; 3 Nephi 12:48; 3 Nephi 27:27. Italics added.

[5]Ephesians 3:11.

[6]*Lectures on Faith* 3:4.

[7]Jeremiah 7:6.

[8]2 Nephi 25:20; 3 Ne. 11:2.

[9]2 Peter 2:1; 1 Corinthians 6:20.

[10]D&C 123:12.

[11]3 Nephi 27:13; D&C 33:12; 39:6.

[12]D&C 45:26; Luke 21:26.

[13]2 Timothy 4:3; 3 Nephi 29:6-7.

[14]1 Nephi 13:39-40.

[15]Acts 1:3.

[16]See scriptural references under the heading "Jesus Christ, Appearances of," in the index to the triple combination, 1981 edition, page 176.

[17]John 15:19.

[18]Deuteronomy 17:6; 19:15; Matthew 18:16.

[19]Jesus, in His mortal ministry, was seen by some as a good man, by others as a deceiver,

by only a few as the Christ; by some as a prophet, and by others as a mere Galilean. Even so, many acknowledged that He spoke with great power, for "never man spake like this man." (John 7:46.)

[20]See D&C 110.
[21]Moses 1:39.
[22]Alma 4:19.
[23]Alma 26:16.
[24]Job 7:4.
[25]3 Nephi 27:27.

2

Even As I Am

With fresh affirmation of the commandment having been given in our time, striving to become like the Father and the Son is more than an optional objective. Focusing on the personality of Jesus is an intellectual and behavioral as well as a theological imperative.

Like His Father, Jesus is perfect in *love, knowledge, power, justice, judgment, kindness, mercy, patience,* and *truth.*[1]

Reflecting upon those eternal attributes with which we are to be seriously and constantly concerned in our lives, we see that the capacity to love is at the very center of the two great commandments.[2] Indeed, the other commandments that follow the two great commandments seem by comparison more like helpful and needed guardrails to keep us on the straight and narrow path! Surely the primacy of love is demonstrated by its recurring appearance in the cluster of commandments.

We note, too, that the attribute of *mercy* is mentioned many times. We read recurringly of *humility* and *meekness.*

13

We encounter as well the stern requirement of *submissive-*
ness. We learn of the constant need for *patience*. We observe
how *kindness, graciousness, gentleness*, and *easiness to be en-*
treated are cited. We see how *justice* is frequently mentioned. We note *judgment's* role, and *wisdom's*.[3]

The need for these and their attending virtues (so much
to be sought after as essential to our happiness here and in
the world to come) has certainly not been kept hidden.
Most of all, in the Master's personality we see these attributes resplendently in action, not just generalized goodness or abstract virtuousness.

To strive to be like Him means that we must be
genuinely serious about developing these same specific
qualities in our own lives: "The disciple is not above his
master: but every one that is perfect shall be as his master."[4]

Joseph Smith noted how long the journey will be—even
for those who in this life earnestly, seriously, and constantly seek to be like Jesus: "When you climb up a ladder,
you must begin at the bottom, and ascend step by step,
until you arrive at the top; and so it is with the principles of
the Gospel—you must begin with the first, and go on until
you learn all the principles of exaltation. But it will be a
great while after you have passed through the veil before
you will have learned them. It is not all to be comprehended in this world; it will be a great work to learn our
salvation and exaltation even beyond the grave."[5]

Jesus, of course, is the only perfect Individual to have
lived upon this earth. There are references to other individuals in the scriptures who were "perfect," but these are
qualified references.[6] Concerning such comparative perfection, the words of Elder James E. Talmage are an appropriate reminder:

"Our Lord's admonition to men to become perfect, even as the Father is perfect (Matt. 5:48) cannot rationally be construed otherwise than as implying the possibility of such achievement. Plainly, however, man cannot become perfect in mortality in the sense in which God is perfect as a supremely glorified Being. It is possible, though, for man to be perfect in his sphere and in a sense analogous to that in which superior intelligences are perfect in their several spheres; yet the relative perfection of the lower is infinitely inferior to that of the higher."[7]

Just as we can move, step by step, from faith to knowledge, so in particular dimensions of living, such as in justice or honesty, some mortals have merited the accolades of prophets "in that thing."[8]

Significantly, when such spiritually advanced individuals were described as perfect, often their "justness" was the virtue cited. Little wonder justice is so stressed, in view of this verse: "He hath shewed thee, O man, what is good; and what doth the Lord require of thee, but to do justly, and to love mercy, and to walk humbly with thy God?"[9] It is clear too that being just not only consists of fair play with one's associates and neighbors, but also reflects largeness of soul. In this broadened sense, "there is not a just man upon earth, that doeth good, and sinneth not."[10]

Jesus Himself did not receive "of the fullness at first," but continued "from grace to grace, until he received a fullness."[11] His progress was incomprehensibly more rapid than ours, but the pathway is the same; so can be the pattern of "grace to grace": "For behold, thus saith the Lord God: I will give unto the children of men line upon line, precept upon precept, here a little and there a little; and blessed are those who hearken unto my precepts, and lend an ear unto my counsel, for they shall learn wisdom."[12]

The perfectability to be sought is not that which some in
this world think can be achieved merely by altering mankind's social, political, and economic systems. Rather, the
gospel sequence is the other way around. Any secular sys-
tem without sufficient human goodness and righteousness
will, sooner or later, fail. We must not mistake mere scaf-
folding for substance.

As in all of the things we learn of Jesus, the insights
available to us, which pertain directly and constantly to our
lives, are incredibly important. For it was He Himself who
posed the question, "What manner of men ought ye to be?"
Answering the question, and being perfect in His humility
but also in truth, He said: "Even as I am."[13] He did not give
us these commands merely to taunt us!

Of His utterance in Matthew 5:48 in which, in humility
and in truth, He did not include Himself as a model of perfection, it was (to use Paul's intriguing phrase) accurate
"for the time then present."[14] It was only after the triumph
of the Atonement and His resurrection that Jesus was fully
perfected: "And he said unto them, Go ye, and tell that fox,
Behold, I cast out devils, and I do cures to day and to morrow, and the third day I shall be perfected."[15]

As we ponder having been commanded by Jesus to become like Him, we see that our present circumstance is one
in which we are not necessarily wicked, but, rather, is one
in which we are so half-hearted and so lacking in en-
thusiasm for His cause—which is our cause, too! We extol
but seldom emulate Him. So much power to do good lies
within our present circumstances that, alas, goes un-
used; so many opportunities go ignored that could bring to
pass much—not a little—righteousness.

Christ's personality, however, is such that throughout
His existence, we see His *love* vigorously and constantly at

work as he gladly used the opportunities at hand. In His first estate, He, as the virtuous volunteer, generously proffered Himself as our Savior. He has responded in love to the opportunities at hand, with the same love, humility, and submissiveness in His second estate, as He actually became our ransom to the Father, paying the price at Gethsemane and Calvary.

Now, having marked and shown the path, He, as our risen and tutoring Lord, waits for us lovingly and personally with open arms to usher us into the third estate. Such is the constancy and kindness of Christ.

Though God's plan and purpose in which Jesus is our Savior is a vast plan, it is also incredibly intimate, making specific demands of us and insuring personal accountability. The fullness of His gospel thus not only denies a man his mistress and a woman "conveniences" like abortion, it raises searching and uncomfortable questions about so many other things that are amiss in our lives—and not just those things that are amiss, but also those that are absent and unaccomplished.

In short, though Christ's message clearly gets in the way of the easy flow of carnal life, as some mortals would like to live it, it opens the only way to a more abundant life here and eternal life hereafter. Being valiant in our testimony of Jesus actually means, therefore, striving to become like Him.

For instance, while the virtue of *patience*, which was fully developed in Him, is never out of season, patience in tribulation will surely be a premiere virtue in the last days. Healthy *self-denial* in which He is the exemplar has always been important, but it is obviously relevant in a time of suffocating selfishness as so many empty their lives of meaning in a wrong-headed search for self-fulfillment.

Submissiveness, in which Jesus showed the way, has always involved tutorial suffering, but this attribute becomes even more important at a time when our individual tutoring will be overlain with the tutoring of a whole people—for purposes wise unto the Lord.

Likewise, as we examine Christ's capacity to love, we observe the fact that He loves us enough to condescend to train us, to help us become what we have the power to become, which is so very much more than we now are. (See Chapter 3.) True love is more than mild regard. True love includes a willingness to teach and to train as parents, for instance, are to do. Thus, as the love of many waxes cold in our time, one of the consequences is the failure to teach and train.

Unlike our love, Jesus' love consists of active restraint as well as pressing encouragement. His perfect love of each and all spares Him the need to accept us as we now are, for He knows perfectly what we have the possibility to become. Mercifully, He did not accept (and leave it at that) Enoch as an inarticulate lad or Moses as a privileged member of Pharaoh's court. There was a city to build and a desert to be crossed, with whole peoples waiting and needing to be led. Therefore, the Father and the Son's love of us is not a passive love that merely watches indulgently over us in our folly. In fact, their love is a pressing love that seeks to correct our folly; it is a determined love that can create an uncomfortable and godly sorrow in us. Remember, Jesus suffered for our sins; He knows perfectly what constructive sorrow we should be experiencing in order to be cleansed. His justice will insist on such needed and cleansing sorrow, for nothing less will do. Because His love of us is true charity, He will not spare us, since to exempt us would be to deny us. It is better that there be sorrow now so that later on there can be a fullness of joy.

Jesus taught us that life consists not in the abundance of the things we possess, but in how rich we are "toward God."[16] Keeping the commandments is vital in our progress toward God—and so is working on each thing that is lacking—as in the case of the good, rich, and noble young man who inquired of Jesus.[17] We too may shrink from such confronting moments, but they will come, and what we lack will be made plainly and painfully clear. We will not be able to say we were not shown and reminded repeatedly. Therefore, as we search the scriptures, our focus should be upon that which will tell us what we must do (to become as He is) and upon that which will stir us so to do. And the very word *search* means from the beginning to the latest unfolding of Holy Writ.

Even the first recorded words of Jesus Christ clearly indicate certain of His attributes. These constitute our earliest clues as to what we must become if we are to be like Him. The very special words appeared in response to the inquiry of the Eternal Father, who, speaking of the need for a Redeemer for us in our second estate, asked, "Whom shall I send?" Standing on that promontory of the unfolding plan of salvation, Jesus replied, "Here am I, send me," revealing Himself as qualified and desirous of submissively serving others.[18] Unsurprisingly, Jesus' premortal characteristics and qualities were to be prominent in His mortal ministry, yet these attributes were part of His character ages before He walked the Holy Land.

And what were His last recorded words as on the cross He ended His mortal ministry? "It is finished." He had meekly and submissively done—perfectly and gloriously—that which He had been sent forth to do. This utterance also tells us of His obedience, His persistence, and His endurance, for in the Joseph Smith Translation we read, "Father, it is finished, thy will is done."[19]

The Savior's supernal service gave Him true and full joy as He gladly attested when, following His resurrection, He visited the lost sheep in the Americas, taught and blessed them, and, weeping twice, said, "And now behold, my joy is full."[20] Therein we see a "finished" Soul who was perfected in His love and obedience, perfected in His capacity to render service.

Christ was completely free of any of the ego considerations we mortals have come to know altogether too well in ourselves and in others. Were our Lord a lesser man, He might have derived pleasure from succulent status instead of joy from service. Were He a lesser being, He might have made a truly exceptional showing in mortality but still not have endured well until all His work was genuinely finished.

There will be another time when He will once again use those same special three words: "It is finished; it is finished."[21] Then in full spiritual celebration of the end of the world, the Lamb of God, who has overcome and who has trodden the winepress alone, will signify the finale of that remarkable achievement—at the center of which achievement is His marvelous love of all and His submissiveness, which brought about the atonement for all.

Meanwhile, as the mortal scene winds down, in His mercy Christ has offered to "stay [His] hand in judgment." We must never forget how He became perfect in His mercy.[22] Meanwhile, though He might overwhelm us in His omnipotence, He has indicated that He lets His works bear witness of Him.[23]

If our emulation of Him is to be serious, amid rampant egoism, we should ponder how, through "all of these things," He was so self-disciplined and how His self-discipline was aided by His *meekness*. Meekness can be a great help to us all in coping with the injustices of life and also in avoiding the abuse of authority and power, to which tendency most succumb—except the meek.

In that premortal council, when Jesus meekly volunteered, saying, "Here am I, send me," it was one of those significant moments when a few words are preferred to many. Never has one individual offered, in so few words, to do so much for so many as did Jesus when he meekly proffered Himself as ransom for all of us, billions and billions of us!

By contrast, in our unnecessary multiplication of words, there is not only a lack of clarity but often an abundance of vanity. Sometimes, too, our verbosity is a cover for insincerity or uncertainty. If there could be more subtraction of self, there would be less multiplication of words.

God's refusal to overwhelm and to conform mankind by His sheer power reflects not only His gentleness but also His justice; He desires to preserve our free agency. The Father and our Savior desire to lead us through love, for if we were merely driven where They wish us to go, we would not be worthy to be there, and surely we could not stay there. They are Shepherds, not sheepherders. If, however, we freely follow—coming, experience upon experience, to be more like Them, knowing the fellowship of Christ's sufferings, and standing our ground in holy places—then will come the resplendent reunion and the unending and ultimate belonging.[24] Meanwhile, we can be sure that holy ground and holy places include the straight and narrow path.

We receive yet another revealing glimpse of divine constraint in the very nature of the voice our Father in heaven used in introducing His Son, Jesus Christ, in the Americas after Jesus' resurrection. Of that gentle voice we read:

"And it came to pass that while they were thus conversing one with another, they heard a voice as if it came out of heaven; and they cast their eyes round about, for they understood not the voice which they heard; and it was *not a harsh voice, neither was it a loud voice;* nevertheless, and *notwithstanding it being a small voice it did pierce them* that did hear to the center, insomuch that there was no part of their frame that it did not cause to quake; yea, it did pierce them to the very soul, and did cause their hearts to burn."[25]

We see this divine concern over preserving our agency in still other ways. Though Jesus knew that Judas would betray Him, yet He did not try to compel him otherwise. At the Last Supper, He did not publicly point an accusing finger at Judas, which would certainly have brought rebuke and scorn from Judas' apostolic peers. We know that Jesus' love was such that He, more than any mortal, would have rejoiced had Judas changed in his heart and forgone the self-chosen role of betrayer. Did not Jesus as Jehovah spare thousands in Nineveh? But Jesus knew Judas' heart and its intent; the rest is a matter of sad record.

Jeremiah described the Lord's justice well: "I the Lord search the heart, I try the reins, even to give every man according to his ways, and according to the fruit of his doing."[26]

Even so, the Lord's commitment to agency is more than gentleness, and it is not indulgent kindness either. It bespeaks a love that recognizes the reality of how true individual growth actually occurs. Everything depends, therefore, upon us and upon our continued openness to spiritual things. Our souls are constantly at risk and in movement. Jesus said we are either increasing or shrinking: "For whosoever receiveth, to him shall be given, and he shall have more abundance; but whosoever continueth not to receive, from him shall be taken away even that he hath."[27]

Jesus' openness to joy and His humility and meekness are equally impressive at every turn. Of the Lord who directed the miracle of the loaves, John recorded, "There came other boats from Tiberias nigh unto the place where they did eat bread, after that the Lord had given thanks."[28] Christ, the fashioner of the miracle of the loaves, actually and genuinely thanked His Father for the bread! It was a real prayer of gratitude, not simply pedagogy to teach His disciples to pray. Christ, the Bread of Life, was thankful for some crusts of bread. Oh, how in attitude as well as in action those of us guilty of the sin of ingratitude must strive to be like Him!

Jesus' townspeople were among the first mortals to witness another dimension of His kindness; they are recorded as marveling, early in His ministry, at his "gracious words"—not alone the carpenter's son's fluency, but also His graciousness.[29] Should it surprise us that it was so, since the Lord is gracious? So it should be with us in our associations and conversations. Graciousness is a dimension of love; it is also practical, for it provides among other things a helpful context for correcting candor when candor is needed.

Is there not deep humility in Him, the majestic Miracle Worker who, nevertheless, acknowledged, "I can of myself do nothing"? Must not Christ's qualities of humility and meekness in relation to our Father in heaven become ours too? Jesus never doubted His power, but He was never confused about its source, either.

Each truth He declared and each trait He displayed mark the way we are to follow. For example, in striving to be more submissive, we must ponder the reality that while

Jesus perfected the attribute of obedience, the process involved exquisite suffering. In our day and in our tongue, the resurrected Jesus described His atoning sufferings as "how sore you know not, how exquisite you know not, yea, how hard to bear you know not."[30] *Exquisite* is defined as *transcending*—but also as *flawless, finished, perfected.* The tempering role of tribulation is thus described—but not only for Jesus.

Likewise, in the midst of our temptations we are reminded that Jesus achieved all that He did even as the adversary afflicted Him, departing, at best, only "for a season." Can we—dare we—ask for immunity from the shaping of righteous suffering when there was none for Him? Or exemption from temptations? He will give us His exceptional grace, but He will not make us exceptions to the required conditions of the second estate.

All such incidents and insights as are provided for us by our Exemplar should both enhance our esteem and love for Him and deepen our own determination amid our own sufferings and temptations. It is overwhelming to know, after what He passed through for us, that we who will have passed through so much less will still find that He waits for us "with open arms."[31] Does not this promised posture signify the blending of His attributes of meekness, mercy, and love?

And when we are weary in well doing, it is reassuring to note that the Father and the Son are working as well as loving Gods. No doubt the latter attribute explains the former. Jesus said, "My Father worketh hitherto, and I work."[32] The imagery, therefore, of working out our salvation is fitting. Besides, we soon learn that the straight and narrow path is neither a freeway nor an escalator. There can be no excellence without effort, and no true love without service. His works witness that it is everlastingly so.

Yet Jesus' meekness was balanced by His justice, as shown in His righteous indignation. In the synagogue, the elders of the establishment saw His look of fierce anger even as He performed a stunning service: "And when he had looked round about on them with anger, being grieved for the hardness of their hearts, he saith unto the man, Stretch forth thine hand. And he stretched it out: and his hand was restored whole as the other."[33]

We who live in a time of ethical relativism see much relative—rather than righteous—indignation. That is all the more cause to marvel at Jesus' unexcelled example.

In His perfected justice and knowledge, Jesus sees "things as they really are." "But the Lord said unto Samuel, Look not on his countenance, or on the height of his stature; because I have refused him: *for the Lord seeth not as man seeth:* for man looketh on the outward appearance, but the Lord looketh on the heart."[34]

Thus, though we may safely repose in God's mercy, yet He, as Jeremiah has said, is perfect in His execution of justice and judgment. It is best that we know what His standards are by which we shall be judged, for the apostle John has observed, His judgment is unvarying and true. Jesus has even said there will be no laws but His laws at His coming.[35] Think upon those sociopolitical implications!

Has not the Lord with equal truth and relevance told us, concerning the resources of this planet, "For the earth is full, and there is enough and to spare"?[36] Should not this reality sober us in terms of what might be achieved as regards to poverty? Clearly, it is the attribute of love, not other resources, that is in short supply—a scarcity that inevitably means misery.

Little wonder, then, that His love and compassion are attributes that underlie the mercy-filled and moving statement: "O Jerusalem, Jerusalem, which killest the prophets,

and stonest them that are sent unto thee; how often would I
have gathered thy children together, as a hen doth gather
her brood under her wings, and ye would not!"[37] Do we not
hear a longitudinal lamentation from Jehovah, now Jesus
of Nazareth, reflecting centuries of insensitivity and unre-
sponsiveness toward Him on the part of ancient Israel?
Whoever constituted the immediate audience the day of
that lamentation, they were, in a sense, stand-ins for earlier
throngs.

As we think of Jesus' role as a shepherd for all on this
planet (and who knows how many more), it is subduing to
ponder His complete compassion and mercy during His
mortal ministry. "But when he saw the multitudes, he was
moved with compassion on them, because they fainted,
and were scattered abroad, as sheep having no
shepherd."[38]

When Jesus told Peter three times to feed His sheep,
what other words of counsel would we expect to come
from Him who is the loving "great and true shepherd"?
Not only does this Shepherd number His sheep, but He
knows and loves them perfectly. He is the perfect
Shepherd.[39]

He not only watches over His sheep today, but prepares
them for the morrow. When Jesus chided a sleepy and
fatigued Peter, James, and John, saying, "Could ye not
watch with me one hour?," surely the memories of that
moment must, in later times, have spurred those three to
sustain "unwearied diligence" in their unfolding
apostleship.[40]

Though Jesus now governs galaxies, yet of a night He
stood by Paul when Paul was in jail. We do not fully understand how Jesus oversees His vast flock and also provides
such individualization in His ministry, but we are coun-

seled: "Believe in God; believe that he is, and that he created all things, both in heaven and in earth; believe that he has all wisdom, and all power, both in heaven and in earth; believe that *man doth not comprehend all the things which the Lord can comprehend.*"[41]

It is one of the hallmarks of human vanity that we assume, because we cannot do something, that God cannot do it either. Is it not marvelous that the Father and the Son blend perfect love and perfect power? Moreover, in the above scripture we see not only that we are to believe in God, but also that we are to believe in what *kind* of God He is—including believing in the attribute cited in this scripture, His omniscience. Peter so understood when, in response to the thrice-put query, "Lovest thou me?," he said, "Lord, thou knowest all things."[42]

We cannot possibly appreciate the majesty and the complexity of the ongoing duties of galactic governance that rest upon Jesus Christ; but as the Shepherd, He did not merely create other worlds and then abandon them. Even so, as the omniscient Creator, He does not rush to tell us things about these other worlds that we neither need to know nor could appreciate. Instead, what He tells us is what we need to know, including that which can reinforce us in our spiritual determination. As immensely important as the truths about the physical universe are, they are not now that which we most need to know. Nephi had the proper sense of proportion: "I know that [God] loveth his children; nevertheless, I do not know the meaning of all things."[43]

Does not God even describe the immensity of the galaxies, the planets, and the stars, in lovable as well as understandable ways? Though He might do so in sweeping technical and astrophysical terms that we could not even understand, He asks us to think in a familial way about faithful Abraham's posterity one day being as numberless as the stars in heaven. What is presented is *beckoning* rather than *overwhelming*. Further, we are asked to view the cosmos as evidence of "God moving in his majesty and power," attesting that, in God's work, souls matter most![44]

God's work is unimaginably difficult work. It is very real, very relentless and repetitive. His course is one eternal round, He has said. But His work is also His glory. And we, His children everywhere, are His work. We are at the center of His purposes and concerns. "We are the people of his pasture, and the sheep of his hand."[45]

Moreover, in the Pearl of Great Price, we read that "millions of earths" would be just a *beginning* to the number of the Lord's creations. However, as Enoch beheld them "stretched out" into space, his awe did not spring from the numerical or spatial dimensions of God's creations but, rather, from the implications underlying those numbers. Enoch responded movingly and with awe—but it was over God's attributes, not His "acreage": "Thou art there [*actuality*], . . . thou art just; thou art merciful and kind forever [*personality*]"![46]

Once we get ourselves straight about our relationship with our Father in heaven and His eternal purposes for us, then perhaps we can know something more about the relationships of the planets and the stars. But these are not of comparatively useful significance for us at the moment.

We need to make constant allowance for the fact that Jesus Christ, in His omniscience, will operate beyond our ken: "For my thoughts are not your thoughts, neither are your ways my ways, saith the Lord."[47] Our mortal ways *are* lower ways.

In affirming Paul's counsel that "our sufficiency is of

God," we are, perhaps without knowing it, acknowledging the grand reality that the Father has made known to us that Jesus Christ is the most intelligent being ever to grace this planet. Indeed, He is not only more intelligent than all other humans combined—He is *perfect* in knowledge.

As we ponder intelligence, a summational strength and attribute of Jesus, it is vital that we understand that intelligence includes more than raw IQ; it includes judgment—and not only in the judicial sense. He who has intelligence, or the light of truth, will forsake completely "that evil one."[48] To forsake the evil one, as Jesus did, is an act of high intelligence and superlative wisdom.

And how laden with meaning are the words chosen by a Jesus perfect in His brilliance as He describes His experiences! For instance, how agonizing it must have been for Christ, who was innocent, to trod the winepress alone. In order to satisfy divine justice, He had to endure "the fierceness of the wrath of almighty God."[49] He had to endure such "fierceness" because, in fact, He had taken upon Him all our transgressions, sins that clearly, grossly, and repeatedly violated the commandments of God; the price had to be paid, a price that we ourselves could not even begin to pay. When, therefore, Christ uses words like *fierceness* and *exquisite* to describe His sufferings, we are left to tremble over that which we cannot fully fathom.

We cannot know, we cannot tell, we cannot appreciate, what those moments must have been like. We do know that it caused Him to bleed at every pore. If His Father required such of *Him*, His Beloved and Only Begotten, we should not be surprised with the seeming fierceness encapsulated in the wintry doctrines as these are applied to our own life experiences.

Throughout the scriptures we find evidence upon evidence of His striking and marvelous personality. We learn of how the Lord of lords and King of kings rules over His creations, which are so vast as to be numberless to us, but not to Him. Yet He says that He will stand in our midst, for we are His people. His governance of galaxies does not prevent His giving us collective and individual attention, just as He watched over nomadic, ancient Israel by day and gave them light by night.

He is not a passive God who merely watches lights on a cosmic computer and presses buttons to implement previously laid plans; He is a personal God who is just, merciful, and kind. His great desire is not to count His creations like so many coins, but to bind up the broken hearts of the inhabitants of each world: sanctification, not quantification, is His work. Has Christ not even promised us that, sooner or later, every soul that forsakes sin shall see His face? Further, that He will appear unto His servants?[50] His desire is to reassure us as directly as we are prepared to receive. Though He is just, He is not exclusionary; His invitations to us are far more numerous than the conditions attached thereto.

Who but merciful and discerning Jesus could be betrayed, arrested, and forsaken, and yet extend to a one-time persecutor, Saul, the great apostolic calling? Later on, the same Creator of this and other worlds stood by a jailed and persecuted Paul in the night.[51]

What other ruler has taken (or would even think of taking) upon Him all the sicknesses and infirmities of His subjects? Who else could say, as did He, "for their sakes I sanctify myself, that they might also be sanctified through the truth"?[52]

His atonement was made feasible because it flowed from His attributes, for He was, as Paul wrote, "obedient unto death." As a part of becoming perfect, however, He "learned obedience by the things which he suffered."[53] Can we, being infinitely less prepared and able, expect to learn obedience in some shortcut way without some suffering?

This remarkable Being describes us lovingly as "the people of his pasture." This Shepherd has surely watched over us—but at so great a cost to Himself! Are we not gladdened and reassured that the Father of our Shepherd "knoweth all things from the beginning," and has prepared "a way to accomplish all his works among the children of men; for behold, he hath all power to the fulfilling of all his words"?[54]

Yes, even His perfection in knowledge is part of His holiness: "O how great the holiness of our God! For he knoweth all things, and there is not anything save he knows it."[55] How merciful is God in His omniscience, which qualities we must not misread. Just as we can ask questions even God cannot answer (How much does love weigh?), so too we can ask God questions for which there are ready answers—but answers for which we are not ready. Pilate asked Jesus, "What is truth?" But the Lord of truth did not deem Pilate ready for or worthy of the answer.

Each of Christ's roles and titles are a "designation with an implication": Redeemer, Messiah, Lord of lords, King of kings, the Author and Finisher of Salvation, Wonderful, Counselor, the Great and True Shepherd, and so on. There is an immense truth contained in each role and title. The designations, such as the Lord God Omnipotent, are worthy of contemplation. Did not King Benjamin urge us to "believe in God . . . believe that he has all wisdom, and all power, both in heaven and in earth"? Even with His omnipotence, however, the Lord God, in His perfect justice, can seal us to Him only if we are "always abounding in good works."[56] And the works we are to do are those things which He did—and of which he told us to go and "do likewise."

The other indicators of the Master's personality are many. Yes, He is boundlessly merciful—but He does require our heart! Yes, He forgives sins—but in His perfect justice He determines whom and how He will forgive. This is not caprice; it is but a reminder to us in our finite perceptions not to second-guess Him who has all the facts and is perfect in mercy and justice. Significantly for us, He forgives those who forgive. Unsurprisingly, these are those who are themselves becoming forgiving—like Him!

So it is that in studying and writing about Jesus, one realizes that in the Savior we are confronted with a real personality—not a person of vague virtues nor of abstract attributes, but *a genuine and real personality*. This latter dimension of His divinity is often subordinated, however unintentionally, to His roles and missions.

Even His wintry doctrines tell us much, not only about His truths enunciated therein, but also about Jesus. One such wintry doctrine with seemingly icy implications is this: "And if thou shouldst be cast into the pit, . . . if the heavens gather blackness, and all the elements combine to hedge up the way; and above all, if the very jaws of hell shall gape open the mouth wide after thee, know thou, my son, that *all these things shall give thee experience and shall be for thy good.*"[57]

There clearly are certain things to be learned by experience "according to the flesh," and our Tutor will not hesitate to immerse us in the needed experiences. Are not all of these, His attributes in action, part of what is called "the testimony of Jesus Christ"?

Jesus' divinity is not only a reality; it is a very directing and drawing reality. We are to "feast upon the words of Christ; for behold, the words of Christ will tell [us] all"—*all*, not some—of the things we should do. And, so often, "what" we are to do is to be learned from the "what" of the Lord we worship. So the truly Christ-centered life is one in which—without being incantational—"we talk of Christ, we rejoice in Christ, we preach of Christ, we prophesy of Christ."[58]

At the gate to heaven, Christ, the King of kings, waits for us with open arms. He awaits not only to certify us, but also to bestow a Shepherd's divine affection upon His sheep as we come Home. The reality that, if we are worthy, we should one day be so warmly received by the Lord of lords and King of kings is marvelous beyond comprehension!

Yet He cannot fully receive us until we fully follow Him. His love for us is unconditional and perfect, but ours for Him is clearly not. Being just, He cannot deviate from His standards by giving us blessings without our obedience to the laws upon which such blessings are predicated. His devotion to truth is such that even in His mercy, He cannot lie, including to Himself, about our readiness. He knows our weaknesses, but, mercifully, He also knows how to succor us as we seek to cope with them. And whatever weaknesses remain in us, He will tutor us and train us to exculpate these, if we will but let Him.

Let others, if they choose, advocate lesser lords or causes for mankind. Only Jesus, truly and fully, advocates the basic and central cause of mankind. Christ's advocacy is advocacy with perfect empathy and mercy. Being sinless Himself, the wounds and scars He bears are actually ours. After all, He was "wounded for our transgressions." He loved us so dearly that He voluntarily laid down His life for us. Furthermore, even though He gives us demanding commandments and stern tasks, He has mercifully promised to prepare a way for us to keep and to fulfill all of them.

Oh, how glorious and wonderful is "this Jesus Christ"!

If contemplating the doing all of these things—to become more and more like Him—makes us feel discouraged, intimidated, and overwhelmed, we need to remember that He never said it all had to be done in a day. Rather, if we could not travel fast, we could at least be steadfast and press forward, doing things in wisdom and order and in a pattern of paced progress, first achieving correct direction and then added momentum. It is the labor of a lifetime and more.

The conditions upon which true joy are based (joy such as He has) are fixed and cannot be altered. It is merely a question of whether or not we wish to come to terms with those conditions—now or later. It is a decision in which, in the justness of God, we are the sole determinants. When we do so decide, we are really in no position to dictate the terms of our own surrender—especially to Him who suffered for our sins, which suffering caused Him to "bleed at every pore."[59]

As we ponder the attributes to be developed and eventually to be perfected, it is helpful to contemplate what happens when we not only lack the desired attributes but, instead, display their very opposites: "And unto thy brethren have I said, and also given commandment, that they should love one another, and that they should choose me, their Father; but behold, they are without affection, and they hate their own blood."[60]

The Lord's indignation is kindled when we refuse to keep the two great commandments, which tell us to follow

Him and to love one another. His indignation is truly aflame when we live without affection for our fellows and hate our own blood. Why? Is it merely because we miss two points on an abstract checklist? Rather, it is because in lacking those attributes, we inflict so much misery upon others and upon ourselves. Furthermore, we thereby follow Satan, the father of misery.[61] We chose not to follow Lucifer once: let us not go back on that decision now!

One important point must be made about the quality of the eternal attributes: In acknowledging His patience or mercy, even when we do it worshipfully, we are only acknowledging mercy and patience as we now know them. His perfection of these two attributes places His mercy and patience (and this is true also with all the other virtues) almost beyond our reach or understanding. The most clear-cut and laudatory act of mercy we have known or the most superlative display of patience within our experience does not even approach His mercy and patience. At best, our degree of development is only "a type and shadow of things which are to come."[62]

True, our experiences tell us what these attributes are, but only as a sample of beautiful carpet tells us what a whole room will be like when so furnished. It is not simply that Jesus has developed all the attributes, but also that He has developed them so completely and perfectly.

If His patience or mercy were like ours, it would not have been sufficient to give Aaron another chance to redeem himself after his errors. If His submissiveness were like ours, then after a few skirmishes with Jewish authorities that tested His obedience to the Father, Jesus would have sought a reasonable settlement instead of marching courageously onto Gethsemane and Golgotha.

To make such allowances for His unique personality, at

least as best we can, marks the difference between the mere admiration of Him and the greater adoration of Him, between verbal veneration and genuine emulation. Verbal veneration is like tipping one's hat and nodding with a smile—instead of falling upon one's knees. In like manner, if we are only mildly responsive to Him, we will stop short of the serious pursuit of His challenge to become like Him.

Only when what *He is* begins to dawn more fully upon us—and to fill us with awe instead of respect—will we really follow Him. Only when what *we are* ponders the many-splendored *"I Am"* can we truly begin to respond to His invitation to follow Him: "And he said unto the children of men: Follow thou me. Wherefore, my beloved brethren, can we follow Jesus save we shall be willing to keep the commandments of the Father?"[63]

Those who say there is danger in regarding Him as so far out of reach as to make following Him an intimidation must recall that the invitation to follow comes *from Him.* The offer of help for that long journey also comes *from Him.* So will the tutoring come *from Him*—for we cannot bear all things yet.[64] All He asks, initially, is that we leave our entangling nets. He will lead us along, line upon line and precept upon precept.

Indeed, when we say that Jesus will "never leave us alone," we intend to say that He will not desert us. But His determination consists of much more than that: He will insistently press upon us the promptings and thoughts and experiences that will be for our good. He will not let us alone when pressing on, instead of pausing, is needed. Or a reminder instead of repose. Or a lesson instead of luxury. Or deprivation instead of accumulation. Or submissiveness instead of selfishness.

In such moments, we will know the Shepherd, not

alone in reassuring and comforting mental imagery of holy scripture, but also in the relentless application of His attributes to our lives. There can be no discounting of His personality then, no waving off of the immense and tugging truth that each of His traits represents, and no relegating of Him to a more relaxed role in our lives. He will not have it. Mercifully for us, He will not have it!

How privileged we are, therefore, when we have "come to a knowledge of the goodness of God, and his matchless power, and his wisdom, and his patience, and his long-suffering towards the children of men."[65]

We do not know with any precision exactly what we "brought with us" from being intelligences as, later on, we become spirit sons and daughters of our Father in heaven. But we can scarcely blame God for our untoward propensities, for it is clear that God did not fashion us *ex nihilo*. Our intrinsic makeup is not His responsibility; there is no such "easy out" in the true gospel of Jesus Christ. Perhaps the input from our intelligence state was a "given" within which God Himself had to work—in which case it would help to explain why this proving estate is so vital and why our obedience to God is so important.

We cannot presume to understand Jesus' relationship with the Father unless we first take account of the fact that Jesus Christ Himself was the great and perfect Emulator, for He "can do nothing of himself, but what he seeth the Father do; . . . for the Father loveth the Son, and sheweth him all things that himself doeth."[66] With Jesus Himself such a careful and observing follower and student of His Father, it is not surprising to read of His paying such careful attention to His followers and His students.

The Father so schooled His Only Begotten Son that through suffering He learned obedience. He was meek and submissive, though egregiously abused: "They have done unto the Son of Man even as they listed."[67] No wonder He made His marvelous petition to the Father: "Glorify thou me with thine own glory which I had with thee before the world was," which gives us an inkling about how it must have been before—when Jesus served *His* apprenticeship by observing all things that the Father Himself had done before Him.[68]

At a divinely determined developmental point, the Father gave all power unto Jesus because of the latter's perfectness and proven righteousness; so all things have been given into Christ's hands. Now He hath "all power according to wisdom, mercy, truth."[69] Even so, He reigns with power according to the will of the Father.

This perfect Student became the perfect Teacher. And we are His students! The invitation is as real as it is imploring:

"Yea, come unto Christ, and *be perfected in him*, and deny yourselves of all ungodliness; and if ye shall deny yourselves of all ungodliness and love God with all your might, mind and strength, then is his grace sufficient for you, that *by his grace ye may be perfect in Christ;* and if by the grace of God ye are perfect in Christ, ye can in no wise deny the power of God."[70]

Footnotes

[1]*Lectures on Faith* 3 and 4. See also Moses 6:6; 1 Nephi 19:9; 2 Nephi 11:5; Alma 42:15.

[2]Matthew 22:37-40.

[3]See the Topical Guide in the LDS edition of the King James Version of the Bible (1979) under such headings as "Gentleness," "Graciousness," "Humility," "Intreated," "Judgment," "Justice," "Kindness," "Love," "Meek, Meekness," "Mercy, Merciful," "Patience," "Submissiveness," and "Wisdom."

[4]Luke 6:40.

[5]*Teachings of the Prophet Joseph Smith* (Deseret Book, 1977), p. 348.

[6]See, for example, Genesis 6:9; 17:1; Matthew 19:21; Ephesians 4:13; Hebrews 12:23.

[7]James E. Talmage, *Jesus the Christ* (Deseret Book, 1977), page 248, note 5.

[8]Alma 32:34; Genesis 6:9; 17:1; Alma 27:27; 50:37.
[9]Micah 6:8.
[10]Ecclesiastes 7:20. See also Romans 3:23.
[11]D&C 93:13.
[12]2 Nephi 28:30.
[13]3 Nephi 27:27. See also Matthew 5:48; 3 Nephi 12:48.
[14]Hebrews 9:9.
[15]Luke 13:32.
[16]Luke 12:15, 21.
[17]See Matthew 19:21.
[18]Abraham 2:27.
[19]John 19:30; JST Matthew 27:54.
[20]3 Nephi 17:20.
[21]D&C 88:106.
[22]D&C 39:18; Alma 7:11-12; Hebrews 2:8; D&C 62:2.
[23]John 5:36; D&C 88:42, 47.
[24]Philippians 3:10; D&C 45:32.
[25]3 Nephi 11:30. Italics added.
[26]Jeremiah 17:10.
[27]JST Matthew 13:10-11.
[28]John 6:23.
[29]Luke 4:22.
[30]D&C 19:15.
[31]Mormon 6:17.
[32]John 5:17.
[33]Mark 3:5.
[34]1 Samuel 16:7. Italics added.
[35]Jeremiah 23:5; John 8:16; D&C 38:22.
[36]D&C 104:17.
[37]Luke 13:34. See also Matthew 23:37; 3 Nephi 10:4-6; D&C 10:65.
[38]Matthew 9:36.
[39]Helaman 15:13; 1 Nephi 13:41; 22:25.
[40]Matthew 26:40; Helaman 15:6.
[41]Mosiah 4:9. Italics added.
[42]John 21:17.
[43]1 Nephi 11:17.
[44]D&C 88:47.
[45]D&C 3:2; Moses 1:39; Psalm 95:7.
[46]Moses 7:30.
[47]Isaiah 55:8.
[48]D&C 93:36-37.
[49]D&C 88:106.
[50]D&C 93:1; 110:8.
[51]Acts 9:5; 23:11.
[52]Matthew 8:17; Alma 7:11-12; John 17:19.
[53]Philippians 2:8; Hebrews 5:8.
[54]Psalm 95:7; 1 Nephi 9:6.
[55]2 Nephi 9:20.
[56]Mosiah 4:9; 5:15.
[57]D&C 122:7. Italics added.

[58]2 Nephi 32:3; 25:26.
[59]D&C 19:18.
[60]Moses 7:33.
[61]Moses 7:37; 2 Nephi 2:27.
[62]Mosiah 13:10.
[63]2 Nephi 31:10.
[64]D&C 50:40.
[65]Mosiah 4:6.
[66]John 5:19-20.
[67]D&C 49:6.
[68]John 17:5; 5:19-20.
[69]Moses 6:61.
[70]Moroni 10:32. Italics added.

3

Ye Are My Friends

Filled with mercy, Jesus generously described his true followers as His friends. Both endearing and lifting, this designation describes how in His perfect love He regards us. He has surely proven His unconditional and unending friendship for us, but we have not yet proven our friendship for Him. He said to His disciples in the meridian of time that they were no longer servants, but friends: "Ye are my friends, if ye do whatsoever I command you."[1]

Attaching this condition does not indicate conditional love for us, since we are loved perfectly by Him. Rather, it describes the condition necessary for us to achieve in order to prove our friendship for Him: we must keep His commandments and strive to become like Him. His truest friends are those who give such evidence of being "valiant in the testimony of Jesus" and who thereby overcome themselves and the world.[2]

The Lord's communications with His prophets reflect a King who would have His subjects also be His friends.

Moreover, His friendship for us is reflected in the *style* as well as the *substance* of His leadership. Centuries ago, "the Lord spake unto Moses face to face, as a man speaketh unto his friend." Centuries later, as the Lord described His creations in presenting an overwhelming vista, He touchingly said, "And again, verily I say unto you, my friends, I leave these sayings with you to ponder in your hearts."[3]

His is a beckoning friendship, a designation that is actually an invitation, for He declared: "I will call you friends, for ye are my friends, and ye shall have an inheritance with me."[4]

We can better understand the remarkable nature of the Lord's friendship for us if we examine His relationship with His prophet-friends in times past.

In no dimension of the divine personality of Jesus Christ do we see His love any more fully expressed than in the divine tutorials given especially to His friends—those who believe in and who strive to follow Him, leaders and followers alike, rich and poor alike, men and women alike, for He is "no respecter of persons." He would not deny these enriching but stretching divine tutorials to any who follow Him, especially those who have already done much to prove their friendship for Him and are thus ready for further lessons.

The manner in which Jesus gives us our individual training indicates He does this work in many ways in order to save and to improve people. Yet His Spirit will not and cannot dwell in unholy temples. And He cannot be deceived; He will have none of the games people play. Hence the individualized tutoring and cleansings, but according to His rules and according to our readiness.

If we ponder the Lord's relationship with Abraham, we see a young man who desired a more righteous and happy life, but who had a lapsing father. Yet this young man genuinely craved the holy priesthood and desired a better way of life. Early in life, well before he was asked to offer Isaac as a sacrifice, Abraham personally experienced a little appreciated lesson: what it was like to contemplate being sacrificed, for the pagan priests actually sought to sacrifice him.[5]

Later, when the time came for offering his own son Isaac in similitude of the Father's offering of Jesus as the supreme sacrifice, Abraham doubtless had unusual empathy for Isaac. But he also had unusual empathy for our Father in heaven—such as could very few, if any, others. Surely Abraham marveled at the submissiveness of his son Isaac, foreshadowing the later and more marvelous submissiveness of Jesus—for whom, however, there was no ram in the thicket!

Abraham and Isaac had undeniable cause for subdued rejoicing in the walk down Mount Moriah, when the latter's sacrifice proved unnecessary. Both had been obedient and submissive, in similitude of that which was to come in the meridian of time. Perhaps there even occurred a special father-and-son conversation, perhaps only rich and instructive silence. But the lesson given to Abraham was not being given to a novice or to an apprentice. The most advanced disciples—far from being immune from further instruction—experience even deeper and more constant tutorials.

When we reflect upon our need for such submissiveness, it is not solely a matter of subordination. Submissiveness involves an invitation to come to grips with reality—to come into harmony with "things as they really are." Only then, proceeding from where one now is, can genuine spiritual progress be made. This is not mysticism, but realism; the acceptance of the truth of things as they were, as they are, and as they will become, as God's purposes for individuals and mankind unfold in the universe.[6] Refusing to look at these realities or shielding our eyes from them— these are signs of immaturity, whereas looking with wide-eyed wonder but with eyes of faith is an act of high intelligence.

Let us consider another whom the Savior loved dearly—Moses, who served the Savior so well in the Sinai and so bravely earlier in the Pharaoh's court. Paul's praise of Moses was not amiss: "By faith Moses, when he was come to years, refused to be called the son of Pharaoh's daughter; choosing rather to suffer affliction with the people of God, than to enjoy the pleasures of sin for a season; esteeming the reproach of Christ greater riches than the treasures in Egypt."[7]

What is the meaning for us of God's stern response to the momentary relapse of noble Moses that prevented his going over Jordan into the long-awaited Promised Land?

Moses, wearied by much murmuring, was nevertheless called upon to importune for yet one more miracle in behalf of his thirsty, badgering people. He cried, "Hear now, ye rebels; must *we* fetch you water out of this rock?" Moses "smote the rock twice: and the water came out abundantly, and the congregation drank, and the beasts also." God honored Moses' authority, even though Moses had momentarily not fully honored God. Apparently Moses, in a brief lapse, arrogated some authority unto himself, indicated by the use of the word *we*, rather than giving full credit and honor to the Lord. There followed a tutorial that was given because Jesus loved Moses. Moses was permitted to view the Promised Land only from atop Mount Pisgah.[8]

Moses, the most meek man upon the face of the earth,[9]

still stood approved of the Lord, but even star pupils need lessons. Indeed, he was sufficiently approved of the Lord that he was later translated.[10] Even so, Moses' tutorials were not finished until they were finished! Such an episode teaches much (perhaps, in a way, more than we now wish we knew) about the tutoring personality of our Savior.

Is this episode not also a lesson for us all about acknowledging, as did Jesus, our continuing dependency upon the Lord lest we too, in fatigue and frustration, arrogate authority to ourselves? And is it not also a lesson for us about how even a virtue already highly developed in us can still require additional attention? Self-sufficiency and selfishness ever require the pruning presence of meekness and humility.

Furthermore, Moses, in that moment on Mount Pisgah overlooking the Holy Land, must have been sobered by the realization that even sterling past performance, when tarnish is present, cannot rob justice of its polishing part.

Three hundred warriors of Gideon could also tell us about the importance of our acknowledging—gladly not grumpily—the hand of the Lord. Before the battle, a swollen army was deliberately reduced by the Lord to only three hundred, "lest Israel vaunt itself," thinking their own hand had saved them.[11] Such episodes cause the soul to shiver as we think of the implications for us in acknowledging the Lord's hand even as we are surrounded by seemingly overwhelming circumstances. Apparently it is necessary for us on occasion to be brought to a white-knuckles point of anxiety so as to be reminded, when rescued, of who our Rescuer is!

Yet mercy is not idle. David, the prophet of such promise, fell, and his portion has been given to another.[12] Even so, we are told that after justice has been satisfied, at some point David will yet be redeemed by God's mercy. God's love balances justice and mercy in divine due process—beside which our mortal due process is, comparatively, either a kangaroo court or an orgy of unredeeming indulgence.

Perhaps these divine tutorials carry such a high priority because the more we are fully developed here, the more chores and opportunities we can be given in the world to come—chores and opportunities that, without growth through tutoring, simply could not be entrusted to us. Perhaps, too, what seems stern, even harsh, as a required experience is merely the necessary crust around the sweetbread of spiritual progress. Little wonder that some such warnings must sometimes come in the form of a shout if they are to save us. A mere frown may not be enough to move us away from a particular precipice.

Imbedded deeply in all of this is an immense and sobering truth about the aloneness that often goes with such soul-stretching experiences. President Brigham Young, who knew by experience the part to be played by tutoring trials, observed with insight that God deliberately does not do everything for man in order that man can learn to act as an independent being "to practice . . . [using] his own resources . . . *to be righteous in the dark* . . . to be a friend of God."[13] President Young's is an illuminating insight. Indeed, we could scarcely face the stern requirements of submissiveness were it not for our knowledge of God's foreknowledge of our capacity to succeed. Was not the Father's "immediate presence" withdrawn in order that Jesus' triumph on the cross could be complete?[14]

When we think of the Savior's mercy, we should remember how often mercy requires patience. And what is patience without time for people to change? Esau's heart was not softened toward Jacob (nor Jacob's toward Esau) the next weekend after their disputed transaction, but only years later when their caravans rendezvoused in the desert and when there was brotherly tenderness and mutual generosity.[15]

While the Savior's tutorials may on occasion be abrupt, these usually occur "in process of time." It is our stubborn use of our agency that slows us, not God's desire for delay. The eternal attributes require time for their development and expression. Instant forgiveness is not always given, though it is desperately wished for. Instant compassion is not always generated, though it is so needed. Alas, empathy for others sometimes waits for its fuller development upon one's passing through the same experience. And, of course, instant patience is a contradiction in terms.

Progress requires time, but time by itself is no guarantor. The scriptures indicate that Methuselah "took glory unto himself," though the infractions are unspecified.[16] Longevity does not automatically produce humility. The mere passage of time does not mean the automatic passing of milestones in personal development.

As for submissiveness, it is both proper and important for us in our afflictions and trials to ask for relief through fasting, prayer, and priesthood blessings. But after all we can do, we then submit to God's will as did Jesus in Gethsemane and on the cross, when, in anguish, He posed aloud the possibility that the cup might pass from Him. On that occasion, the key word that expressed Jesus' attribute of submissiveness was "nevertheless."

Paul thrice petitioned God that the unidentified thorn of affliction might be taken from Him. The answer was "no." In place of full relief came God's grace.[17] We express our desires out of an imperfect perception, and upon learning the Father's desires, we yield to His eternal perspective and purposes. It is the only surrender that is also a victory!

Examining yet another tutoring friendship, we see a prolonged pattern of instruction in the relationship of Jesus with Enoch.[18] In the beginning, Enoch felt inadequate. But, happily, he was meek and teachable. We see a highly empathic Enoch when his bowels were filled with mercy for all humankind. He saw the impact of sin and wickedness upon his people and wondered aloud just how long-suffering a merciful God could be. An Enoch disconsolate over the destructiveness of sin encountered the rich redemptiveness of God.

Enoch surely had received special lessons in patience in the development of his special city "in process of time." Though His enemies hated and feared the city of Enoch, they nevertheless stood "afar off" out of respect for Enoch's access to divine power, which access depended upon Enoch's personal righteousness.

As a result of his tutorials, the Enoch who had earlier felt inadequate later actually moved mountains. A matured Enoch, once slow of speech, became so powerful the people trembled when he spoke, "so great was the power of the language which God had given him." But Enoch never forgot the Source of his eloquence.

In the city of Enoch, we also observe the Lord producing a particular kind of people—a righteous people "of one heart and one mind" who had no poor among them. It was the outcome that the Lord has always desired and that has been achieved (and sustained) only this once in human history.

Yet it all began with a meek lad who was slow of speech and who was disliked by the people.

Centuries later, President Brigham Young, who was no stranger either to the tutorials the Lord gives to his friends, spoke of a particular time, after the original latter-day Twelve were named and called, when these "friends" of Jesus in this dispensation went through a seeming period of humiliation wherein the Twelve felt left out, or at least not fully used, by Joseph Smith. To what extent this reflected divine deliberation we do not know. We do know, however, that later on, the nine most-tutored members of the Twelve were those valiants who participated in the mission to the British Isles and other soul-stretching tests, and who later carried off the Kingdom to the valleys in the tops of the mountains. They were the Lord's proven leaders, having "in process of time" gained confidence in their capacity to do whatever the Lord asked them to do. They had learned with Nephi that special trusting submissiveness: "I will go and do the things which the Lord hath commanded, for I know that the Lord giveth no commandments unto the children of men, save he shall prepare a way for them that they may accomplish the thing which he commandeth them."[19]

Trusting in the Lord is so vital! Yet it is seldom a quality that is fully in place in Jesus' "friends" at the very beginning.

Do we not, where record was made, likewise learn of Jesus' working with certain of the original Twelve in His day in a manner that developed them individualistically by taking into account their particularized needs? Presently, however, we know precious little concerning the other members of the original Twelve. What do we now know, for instance, about the personality or apostolic service of Thaddeus or of Simon the Canaanite? Nor is the record complete concerning Barsabas, surnamed Justus, who, along with Matthias, was honored by being nominated for membership in the Council of the Twelve to fill the vacancy that existed after the betrayal and death of Judas.[20] Though Matthias was chosen, presumably Barsabas continued faithful and effective in the work, for the Lord loved him as much as He loved Matthias. Likewise, we may wonder about later developments in the life of Nicodemus, or about the Nephite apostles who are named but about whom we are told virtually nothing individually.

This observation is made not by way of complaint but by way of quiet anticipation. We should assume that these remarkable men were "no less serviceable"—and also no less tutored—than their prophetic brethren about whom we know somewhat more. For example, of Moroni we are told: "Behold, he was a man like unto Ammon, the son of Mosiah, yea, and even the other sons of Mosiah, yea, and also Alma and his sons, for *they were all men of God*. Now behold, Helaman and his brethren were *no less serviceable* unto the people than was Moroni; for they did preach the word of God, and they did baptize unto repentance all men whosoever would hearken unto their words."[21]

And do we not see different gifts manifested by those whom Jesus calls His friends? Did not John the Baptist receive high commendation from Jesus, even though John performed "no miracle"?[22]

Just as Jesus, in a customized manner, tutored such ancients as Enoch, Moses, Peter, and Paul, surely He has done likewise in this dispensation with those whom He has called to lead in His Kingdom. And what He does for one, He does for all of His children who are willing followers. Discerning enough to know all our individual needs, strengths, and weaknesses, He is willing to train us in such a way that those weaknesses can be overcome or can even be made into strengths.

An incident, seemingly small, gives yet another large

indication of Jesus' kindness and encouraging ways as our Teacher. Luke reported the episode more briefly, but Matthew, one of the Twelve, included Jesus' full reply in which the Master reassuringly told the original Twelve they would one day judge the twelve tribes of Israel. This generous and encouraging indicator is all the more significant because it was given just after Peter's human and candid observation to Jesus about how much the Twelve had sacrificed and had given up to follow Him.[23]

There were apparently conversational asides in which Jesus taught His closest disciples. Privately, He observed on one occasion how blessed they were to hear and see the things they were hearing and seeing.[24] For those of us living in these days of prophecy fulfilled, can we not muster more gratitude than we now do for what we are privileged to see?

Furthermore, just as we see Jesus as the perfect example, we also see how some are used as less than perfect examples—as people, like us, in process of becoming better. One day, for instance, we shall know more about Jonah and his eagerness for vindication. A repentant Nineveh was mercifully not destroyed, which provided a great lesson not only in the tutoring of one prophet, but for us all, concerning the principle of mercy.[25] Mercy rejoices in every step toward righteousness and is not offended by being pleasantly surprised. Though he acknowledged God's graciousness, mercy, and kindness, Jonah had not fully understood the application of these attributes. Has not God even referred to His Plan of Salvation as the *plan of mercy*?[26]

The marvelous capacity Christ has to blend reproof and reassurance is yet another reflection of His perfect love. Instead of scolding and repudiating Thomas, who said he would not believe in Jesus' resurrection *except* he could see and feel the wounds in Jesus' body, Jesus gave him his desires. But, at the same time, He reminded us that true faith does not require such absolute proof.[27] Unlike Thomas, some of us ask not only for absolute proof, but also for its perpetual renewal, contradicting the Father's plan by which, essentially, we are to walk by faith and triumph by faith.

Jesus' patience is clearly evident as He prepared the Twelve for His crucifixion and resurrection and for their own temporary scattering. The Twelve kept assuring Jesus they believed. Once He asked searchingly, "Do ye now believe?," and went on to observe how they would be scattered. He even foretold where they would meet Him again, saying that after His resurrection He would go before them into Galilee. He told them that their overwhelming grief would, nevertheless, be followed by much joy. Though carefully instructed, Peter and John, after seeing the empty tomb, went away wondering.[28]

We can expect to do some wondering too. We will not understand everything at once, nor all the truths we are taught. Our righteousness and our readiness are determining factors more often than we know as to what we understand.

Though Jesus spoke to the Twelve of the crucifixion and resurrection several times, the Twelve still did not fully understand:

"Then he took unto him the twelve, and said unto them, Behold, we go up to Jerusalem, and all things that are written by the prophets concerning the Son of man shall be accomplished. For he shall be delivered unto the Gentiles, and shall be mocked, and spitefully entreated, and spitted on: And they shall scourge him, and put him to death: and the third day he shall rise again. *And they under-*

stood none of these things: and this saying was hid from them, neither knew they the things which were spoken."[29]

The deep love and respect they felt for Jesus may have made the Twelve reluctant to ask Him about that which He had said—especially about the death and resurrection. Since never before had there been a resurrection, the conceptual inadequacy of the Twelve was understandable.

How patient Jesus was as the Master Teacher—with how very good but far less than perfect students. Is this example of patient persistence not one that we, whether as pupil or teacher, are to contemplate and to implement, time and again, in our lives? Will we be sufficiently trusting and patient as we teach others, or as we must wait upon the Lord for fullness of understanding concerning that which we too have been taught but do not yet comprehend? If we can trust the answers God has already given, why not the answers yet to be given, including patiently awaiting the data from our first estate that will illuminate the imponderables of our second estate?

Impatience is not only abrupt but destructive, leaving its own human debris, as in the case of the children of Israel who, while Moses was on Mount Sinai, relapsed by making a golden calf to worship. It seemed they could not wait even a few more days when Moses "delayed to come down." This episode underscores the need not only for general patience, but also for patient trust in the Savior and in His prophets, even in those circumstances when we feel neglected or miffed—when, for instance, the Brethren seem inexplicably to delay. Keeping ourselves spiritually intact is *our* responsibility lest we too be "turned aside quickly out of the way."[30] But when we stay in the way, Christ gives us rich and reassuring experiences.

Though elsewhere we read of Jesus giving a reminding

look to one disciple,[31] we also see His gladness and graciousness as His countenance smiled upon others of His
disciples:

"And it came to pass that Jesus blessed them as they did
pray unto him; and his countenance did smile upon them,
and the light of his countenance did shine upon them, and
behold they were as white as the countenance and also the
garments of Jesus; and behold the whiteness thereof did
exceed all the whiteness, yea, even there could be nothing
upon earth so white as the whiteness thereof."

It occurred a second time: "And when Jesus had spoken
these words he came again unto his disciples; and behold
they did pray steadfastly, without ceasing, unto him; and
he did smile upon them again; and behold they were white,
even as Jesus."[32]

Though He tutors them, Jesus loves and, therefore,
consistently honors and sustains His prophets: "Behold, I
do not destroy the prophets, for as many as have not been
fulfilled in me, verily I say unto you, shall be fulfilled. And
because I said unto you that old things have passed away, I
do not destroy that which hath been spoken concerning
things which are to come."[33]

Jesus' mortal ministry was elaboration, not rejection;
fulfillment rather than annulment; a building up, not a
tearing down of that which His own prophets had so
painstakingly written and declared.

Along with occasional needed reproof, Jesus praised
His prophets; how marvelous for any prophet to have
Jesus say this of Him: "And now, behold, I say unto you,
that ye ought to search these things. Yea, a commandment
I give unto you that ye search these things diligently; *for
great are the words of Isaiah.*"[34]

How reassuring was Jesus' love to another prophet who
fretted over the inadequacy of his own words:

"Thou hast also made our words powerful and great, even that we cannot write them; wherefore, when we write we behold our weakness, and stumble because of the placing of our words; and I fear lest the Gentiles shall mock at our words. And when I had said this, the Lord spake unto me, saying: Fools mock, but they shall mourn; and my grace is sufficient for the meek, that they shall take no advantage of your weakness; and if men come unto me I will show unto them their weakness. I give unto men weakness that they may be humble; and my grace is sufficient for all men that humble themselves before me; for if they humble themselves before me, and have faith in me, then will I make weak things become strong unto them."[35]

The divine attributes of power and knowledge follow upon our adequate development of the other attributes and sufficient righteousness so that we can, for instance, be safely entrusted with heavenly power. Knowledge, in its fullness, will not only induce genuine effort to learn all we can about *truth*, especially saving truths while in this second estate, but must also wait upon the restoration of our premortal memories and such other bestowals as may accompany our resurrected status. But meanwhile, we cannot be disdainful of gaining more knowledge or be careless in our use of present power.

As one ponders Jesus' greatness—nay, His perfectness—it is breathtaking to see His attributes at work; but it is also overwhelming!

Did Jesus not understand that we would, at times, feel intimidated by the very perfectness of His life? Of course He knew and knows! His omniscience—perfect knowledge—about the long developmental distance we have to travel only makes His entreaties and invitations to us all the more significant and encouraging.

He understands completely! Hence, His assurances are

completely reliable; He will lead us along, giving us here a little, there a little. He knows perfectly our bearing capacity as well as our individual distances yet to be traveled.

Jesus' kindness and concern for His disciples can be noticed in His efforts to help them establish a wise pace even in their diligence. The wise use of time helps to fit us for eternity. On one occasion, when the Twelve had given their personal reports to the Savior, He could see how harried and wearied they were.[36] When the press of the crowd upon them was so great that they could scarcely eat, Jesus took them apart to rest for awhile in a solitary place. Who more than the Lord of the Sabbath understands about the need for rest?

Happily, his foreknowledge of our failures does not cause Christ to give up concerning us without providing us with the opportunity to repent and to follow Him. His foreknowledge rests upon His perfect awareness of our weaknesses and capabilities, while His relentlessly re-deeming love makes of Him a true and perfect Shepherd.

The Father's entire plan of salvation has taken into ac-count beforehand our prospective successes and failures, so that His plan will be fully executed and His purposes completely fulfilled through Christ. Unlike us, God can see the end from the beginning, "and thus it is"![37]

Thus we are to "confess" God's hand "in all things."[38] This clearly does not mean that He causes or approves of all things that occur; rather, it means that He has taken all things into account from the beginning, and His purposes will still prevail. A failure to confess this is a failure to ac-knowledge God's attributes of omniscience and omnipo-tence—another example of not knowing "what we wor-ship." Such is evidence of defective faith in a defective deity—like saying a god exists but does not preside, cares but cannot deliver, and has identity but not sovereignty.

One searches in vain for accurate analogies to portray what it is like for us in our own imperfections to ponder His perfections; clearly it is not for finiteness to comprehend infiniteness. For, in addition to believing in God, we are counseled to accept His omniscience, to believe "that man doth not comprehend all things which the Lord can comprehend."[39]

Likewise, when the Lord asks us to confess His hand in all things, He is not seeking our ritualistic incantation concerning His powers. Again, He is after realism in us, including our acknowledgment that His omniscience has made allowance even for human errors of which He does not approve, but which are not allowed to frustrate His overall plan. We can count on His plans—even when He cannot count on us!

Our mistakes call forth the moments of reproof and correction that surely come to us, if we are *humble* enough to receive them. Did not a truth-telling prophet candidly remind a mighty, ego-encrusted King Saul that in an earlier time, "thou wast little in thine own sight"? Out of that very episode came a great statement on submissiveness: "And Samuel said, Hath the Lord as great delight in burnt offerings and sacrifices, as in obeying the voice of the Lord? Behold, to obey is better than sacrifice, and to hearken than the fat of rams." Saul, not without greatness, then acknowledged that he had erred because he "feared the people, and obeyed their voice,"[40] a circumstance not unlike that which Aaron experienced by listening briefly to *vox populi* instead of *vox Dei*. Even in this democratic age, the first great commandment still means what it says.

As we brush against each other in the day-to-day work in His kingdom, which is put in place "for the perfecting of the Saints," we sometimes assume we are better informed than we are. There comes to mind the experience of a less-than-fully-informed Moroni, who mistakenly concluded that another Church leader, Pahoran, was not doing enough in the stressful circumstances of civil war. Pahoran's meek response to his "beloved brother," Moroni, was not the last such reassurance that will be needed in the work of the Kingdom.[41] Along with miscommunications are the feelings of being left out. Even John the Baptist, in whom there had been "no greater prophet," needed reassurance.[42]

Being a true friend, Jesus customizes His communications to us for reasons of our readiness and need—and for divine tutorial purposes that we cannot always discern. Jesus reassuringly told an imprisoned Paul what his itinerary was: Rome was next! Yet He left a lonely , but trusting, Moroni with some uncertainty as to the likely length of his loneliness. Moroni wrote: "Behold, my father hath made this record, and he hath written the intent thereof. And behold, I would write it also if I had room upon the plates, but I have not; and ore I have none, for *I am alone.* My father hath been slain in battle, and all my kinsfolk, and I have not friends nor whither to go; and how long the Lord will suffer that I may live I know not."[43]

Yet Moroni realized that he was watched over by Him who was perfected in His sensitivity to aloneness. Did not a wayfaring Jesus once lament that "the foxes have their holes, and the birds of the air nests; but the Son of man hath not where to lay his head"?[44]

There are other associational costs of discipleship. Alma forsook his wealth to follow and then was "rejected by those who were once his friends and also by his father and his kindred"—a contrast to a good man in Jerusalem who lacked that one thing: the capacity to forsake his wealth and follow Jesus.[45] It is only within this very zone of our deepening trust of Him who has called us His friends that there can be a satisfactory resolution of the seeming perplexities growing out of the apparent collision of man's free will and the foreknowledge of God. With obedience borne of lengthy experience with the Lord, but without all the data concerning all the later events that would make his tedious and extra work useful, Mormon, that superlative editor, nevertheless prepared auxiliary plates. The Spirit of the Lord had entreated him, whisperingly, that there was "a wise purpose" in so doing. Significantly, Mormon added: "And now, *I do not know all things;* but *the Lord knoweth all things* which are to come; wherefore, *he worketh in me to do according to his will."*[46]

Such is the trust that we need in God's omniscience, causing us to be entreated, freely, into participating in His purposes—and without fretting. Such trust allows us to be concerned with making a good choice rather than brooding over whether or not we had a choice. Besides, if we cannot accept and trust in the Lord's declaration that He has left us "free to choose," in which of His other declarations can we then trust? Being now limited in our information and limited in our perception, it is a good time to trust God!

As the object of the shaping, we can scarcely be expected to understand everything in the sculpturing of our souls. In our imperceptivity, we may, for instance, believe we are already quite symmetrical in certain portions of our personality, only to encounter an experience in which God suddenly and publicly shears off a whole encrustation. We had not even noticed the need, but we feel the pain; perhaps we were too pleased with our lives.

In acknowledging that we cannot comprehend all that God comprehends, this attitude should not apply alone to the galaxies, but also to the constellation of characteristics that make up our present personalities.

Did Peter, who once thought himself more ready for

rigorous events than he was, know that his vouchsafing (saying that he would never deny the Savior) would require the dramatic learning episode that followed? Excruciatingly painful as it was, in the judgment of God it was necessary. Peter did not comprehend what God comprehended about his developmental needs, including what is certitude and what is not. As the cock crowed for the third time, Peter courageously began to face reality, a poignant reminder about how the Lord's omniscience both knows things about us that we do not know and then does something about these things—if we are willing. Besides, Peter had yet before him these experiences for which he was being prepared:

"But before all these, they shall lay their hands on you, and persecute you, delivering you up to the synagogues, and into prisons, being brought before kings and rulers for my name's sake. And it shall turn to you for a testimony. Settle it therefore in your hearts, not to meditate before what ye shall answer."[47]

These events would require genuine certitude, and any prematurity of response was to be avoided.

If some pride needs to be peeled off, off it comes, but in a time and manner that our Tutor thinks best. We will feel that pain, shame, and dismay. But if we can trust Him who is doing the sculpturing of our soul—even in the midst of "all these things"—we have developed some of that submissiveness which is so necessary in our further development. Usually, the more the truth is concerned with our personal developmental needs, the greater the possible pain or offense to our self-image. Hence the vital need for humility.

So it is that the general proving process of mortality is really the stunning sum of its billions of individual subsets, all of which is overseen by an all-knowing and all-loving

Father and Son. But, though overseen by them, we must, through the mists of the moment, keep our eyes on them; there is actually nowhere else to look.

In the midst of one illustrative experience, Jesus challenged His friends, the Twelve: "Will ye also go away?" Then came the marvelous reassurance from humble Simon Peter: "Lord, to whom shall we go? thou hast the words of eternal life. And we believe and are sure thou art that Christ, the Son of the living God." What was taught by Jesus on this occasion included His observation, "Have not I chosen you twelve, and one of you is a devil?"[48] This was not taught out of bitterness or to demean the Twelve. Rather, He was reminding them, even in the midst of their loyalty, that they should understand that He knew one among them would betray Him, the Savior. How often in the months and years to follow might the faithful eleven apostles have reflected on that moment? Not in perpetual indignation over disloyal Judas—but in a deepening respect of the divine foreknowledge of Jesus for whom they were the special witnesses!

Though the Eleven—echoing King Benjamin's counsel—knew they could not comprehend all that Jesus comprehended, they were trusting. It is unlikely, indeed, that they worried over Judas' free will; it is certain they anguished and were saddened over his misuse of it.

As one ponders attributes like meekness and humility, he cannot help but observe how much of our mortality is spent in rearranging the furniture of our relationships and in interminable organizational shufflings because of ego rather than for genuine improvement. How many new emphases and new thrusts are simply new extrusions of untamed ego? Or represent a drunkenness of conscientiousness?

Instructive, indeed, is that circumstance in which the

believing mother of James and John unmeekly pressed the Savior in behalf of her sons, hoping they might later sit on his right hand and on his left hand. Jesus, who *was* meek, did not reprove the worshipful and good mother, but spoke truthfully to her, saying she did not realize what she asked.[49] Her petition resembled so many of our prayers; we do not realize the implications of what we ask. Furthermore, Jesus noted that this particular decision was His Father's anyway. Later that day, He further taught ten indignant apostles (presumably James and John as well) about being servant-leaders.

If, therefore, we truly want the best for our sons and daughters, we would want for them—not status—but more *meekness, mercy, love, patience*, and *submissiveness*.

Several times concern arose over precedence among the Twelve—one time with some "strife." Another episode involving Jesus' effort to disabuse His disciples about status occurred in connection with His final Passover feast. Again, He stressed to the Twelve their leader-servant role. Finally, having washed the feet of the Twelve, Jesus pleaded with the original Twelve to love one another as He loved them. Likewise, the Nephite Twelve were carefully counseled against having doctrinal and other disputations among them.[50]

Surely Jesus has given us the model of the leader-servant in which the pattern evokes, "How can I help?", not "How can I help myself?" The leader-servant is perfectly epitomized by Jesus, and if we are to become like Him, so it must be with us.

Indeed, the very usefulness of our lives depends upon our willingness to serve others:

"But Jesus called them unto him, and said, ye know that the princes of the Gentiles exercise dominion over them, and they that are great exercise authority upon them. But it shall not be so among you: But whosoever will be great among you, let him be your minister; and *whosoever will be chief among you, let him be your servant:* Even as the Son of man came not to be ministered unto, but to minister, and to give his life a ransom for many."[51]

Can we expect to become like Him, given our imperfections, unless we can learn to accept and apply needed reproof and correction such as was given in the episodes noted? How essential our capacity to receive correction and reproof is, for "he that refuseth instruction despiseth his own soul: but he that heareth reproof getteth understanding."[52] Deserved self-esteem depends upon our meekness.

In our personal development, the emery wheel of events can polish us, and the sandpaper of circumstances can smooth us. Too often, when so worked upon, we grow fearful instead of being trusting and submissive. But Peter overcame his fearfulness, and so can we.

Too often we behave as if we were in massive competition with others for God's love. But we have His love, unconditionally and universally; it is our love of Him that remains to be proven, such as through service to others. Magnanimity, after all, arises from meekness.

We are often overly concerned, for instance, with our acquiring or holding turf when, in fact, we are urged instead to let go of the things of the world. Any possessiveness for the things of this world is a wasted effort, for it is obviously on a collision course with reality. One's claims to turf will have no legal status in the kingdom of heaven anyway. It is, for example, our degree of attained meekness or patience—not our title to property or position—that will "rise with us in the resurrection" and will live on.

In seeking to demonstrate our friendship for the Savior,

we cannot invoke, much as we might like to, the excuse
that life was once much simpler, such as in the period of
Jesus' mortal ministry. If anything, there are more than
enough parallels between His time and ours to make it clear
that circumstances are roughly and sufficiently compara-
ble; so will be the tutorials. Therefore, in appealing to divine justice, we should be very careful indeed in the midst
of common temptations about invoking circumstantial
pleadings.

Nor does Jesus' influence on the tutored depend upon
His personal proximity. The Comforter will teach us and
strengthen us. After the ascension of the resurrected Jesus,
the fullness of his apostolic ministry began to settle in upon
Peter, who, far from shrinking from open acknowledgment of his acquaintanceship with the Savior, became
(subsequent to the bestowal of the gift of the Holy Ghost
and the ascension of Jesus) emboldened and courageous.

When Peter and John went together to the temple to
teach, they blessed a lame man who was made to walk "in
the name of Jesus Christ of Nazareth."⁵³ This miracle oc-
casioned the gathering on Solomon's Porch of a multitude
who then were taught by Peter and John. Peter chided
those present who had denied Jesus Christ in the presence
of Pilate and who had preferred Barabbas to Jesus. However, he exhibited the same spirit of forgiveness shown by
the Savior, observing that what had been done earlier had
been done in ignorance.

Thus we see not only an emboldened but also a
sweetened Peter emulating the Savior's qualities of merciful healing and forgiving. Before the Sadducees laid hands
upon Peter and John that day, five thousand people believed two obscure fisherman! Did Peter and John, per-
chance, remember on that day how their Master taught
another multitude of five thousand?

When arraigned later before Ananias, the high priest, and Caiaphus, Peter may have been stirred by still other memories as he declared by what power the lame man had been healed. It had been done by the power of Christ—whom they had wantonly crucified!

Now, as Peter and John stood before the council, it was a brave and moving moment, and as the *illuminati* "saw the boldness of Peter and John and perceived that they were unlearned and ignorant men, they marvelled." The council went into executive session and then threatened Peter and John, instructing them to "speak henceforth to no man" in the name of Christ. At once came that courageous and classic reply from Peter and John: "Whether it be right in the sight of God to hearken unto you more than unto God, judge ye. For we cannot but speak the things which we have seen and heard." Fearing the people, the council again threatened them and let the apostles go.[54]

It should not offend us, therefore, to see even great men growing and developing. Nor should we be offended to see the growth in ourselves as we move, grace by grace, from what we are to what we have the power to become.

On every hand, we see in the divine tutorials of the Lord given to His friends how this mortal experience—in order for us to reach the Father's high purposes for His children—could not consist of anything resembling play acting in which we go winkingly through the motions of stress, testing, and proving. The tutorials must be real, or the learning would be superficial.

It was so even for the Son, who, so much more than the rest of us, knew what lay ahead of Him and what the implications were of his every test and trial. With assurance as well as anticipation, He said to the Twelve, "I have overcome," even *before* He had experienced the fullness of the agonies of the Atonement. He asked that, if possible, the cup might pass from Him. Still later, He cried out, feeling forsaken.[55]

Do we need more validation as to the complete realness of his proving experience? Or how in earnest God is about all of us and our individual tutorials?

God's tutoring of us is relentless even in its gradualness. Jesus observed, for instance, that when one is not willing to carry his own cross and come after Jesus, he cannot be Jesus' disciple.[56] But quiet persistence depends on our obedience, taking up the cross daily.

How vital it is that we do what Jesus urged: "Settle this in your hearts, that ye will do the things which I shall teach, and command you."[57] Did not Peter, who knew whereof he spoke, declare that after the faithful follower had "suffered a while," God would "settle" him?[58] To carry our cross does require settled and genuine faith, including faith in the eventual feasibility of the Lord's call for us to be like Him, virtue by virtue and attribute by attribute.

So, while the Master repeatedly said that we are to follow in His footsteps, it is not as if we were headed toward some *geographical* destination but, rather, toward a *developmental* destination.

When the jarrings and the weariness come, or the sudden shocks, if we can maintain this perspective about tutoring, we can be seen through the difficulties of the moment. Nor should we be surprised if, having passed one test well, another seems to come so quickly. Was it not so for Him? He did not get three months off after the three great temptations or a weekend at the seashore after delivering the Sermon on the Mount. He was not allowed to extend His triumphal entry into Jerusalem into a year-long celebration. Quickly, so quickly, the realities of what He next had to do bore down upon Jesus.

So it is with us. If the Lord, in His love for us, presses things in upon us with rapidity as well as relentlessness, and if we feel crowded, perhaps we really are being crowded—but for our own sakes, and so that our "performance" can be consecrated "for the welfare" of our souls.[59]

Later on, we will be grateful for the compression and sheer volume of the challenges, but right now, the volume is a vexation. Therefore, how great and continuing is our dependency upon the Lord, which is one of the first and fundamental facts of life, never to be forgotten, even when we are making genuine progress.

No wonder Jesus prayed so to the Father. And oh, how He prayed, *never* forgetting to call upon the Father. In this, too, Jesus was unique. Even the very righteous brother of Jared, a truly remarkable man, once was chastised during a visitation from the Lord because he "remembered not to call upon the name of the Lord."[60] How vital prayer is, therefore, for all of us! How vital it is that even our "busyness" in doing His work not crowd out our prayers to our Father.

We, naturally and properly, petition according to our needs. He, however, in His perfect knowledge and love, will assess our needs according to that which is right for us.[61] Would we really want it any other way, knowing how He regards and loves us?

Footnotes

[1]John 15:14-15.
[2]D&C 79:79; 121:29.
[3]Exodus 33:11; D&C 88:62.
[4]D&C 93:45.
[5]Abraham 1:2, 7; 2:5.
[6]D&C 93:24.
[7]Hebrews 11:24-26.
[8]Numbers 20:10-11, italics added. See also Deuteronomy 1:37; 3:26.
[9]Numbers 12:3.
[10]Alma 45:19.

11See Judges 7.
12D&C 132:38-39.
13Brigham Young's secretary's journal, January 28, 1857. Italics added.
14See Talmage, *Jesus the Christ*, p. 661.
15Genesis 33.
16Moses 8:3.
17See 2 Corinthians 12:7-10.
18See Moses 6:27–7:69.
191 Nephi 3:7.
20Acts 1:21-26.
21Alma 48:18-19. Italics added.
22John 10:41.
23Matthew 19:27-29.
24Luke 10:23-24.
25See Jonah 4.
26Alma 42:15.
27John 20:24-29.
28John 16:31-32; Matthew 26:31-32; John 20:10.
29Luke 18:31-34. Italics added.
30See Exodus 32.
31Luke 22:61.
322 Nephi 19:25, 30.
333 Nephi 15:6-7. See also Matthew 5:17; D&C 10:52.
343 Nephi 23:1. Italics added.
35Ether 12:25-27.
36Mark 6:31.
371 Nephi 9:6.
38D&C 59:21.
39Mosiah 4:9.
40See 1 Samuel 15.
41See Alma 60.
42Matthew 11:2-4, 11.
43Mormon 8:5. Italics added.
44Matthew 8:20.
45Alma 15:16; Mark 10:21.
46Words of Mormon 1:7. Italics added.
47Luke 21:12-14.
48John 6:68-70.
49See Matthew 20:20-28.
50Luke 22:24; John 13:31-35; 3 Nephi 11:28; 18:34.
51Matthew 20:25-28. Italics added.
52Proverbs 15:32.
53Acts 3:6.
54See Acts 4:1-22.
55John 16:33; Matthew 27:46.
56Matthew 10:38; Luke 9:23; 14:27.
57JST Luke 14:28.
581 Peter 5:10. See also Colossians 1:23.
592 Nephi 32:9.
60Ether 2:14.
613 Nephi 18:20.

4

Go, and Do Thou Likewise

Becoming like Jesus Christ requires doing the things He did—exclusive, of course, of those things He accomplished that were utterly unique to Him. The episodes or teachings selected for this chapter tell us some of those things concerning which we are instructed to "Go, and do . . . likewise."[1]

To begin with, we can scarcely become like Jesus if we do wrong things or fall away, and a common cause of falling away is temptation. We are to "do likewise" regarding temptation, for the cease-and-desist requirements of gospel living are as vital as the start-and-persist portions.

Examining the temptations of Christ can be very instructive, particularly what we know about His forty days in solitary seclusion. There, while fasting and praying, He met temptations beyond those we can imagine. Even so, He set a pattern for us in surmounting temptation. Without our doing likewise, we could scarcely begin to be like Him.

Elder James E. Talmage asserts authoritatively that the realization that He was, indeed, the Messiah came to Jesus gradually. As a lad, He knew He was the Son of God. Yet as He grew, grace upon grace, and in wisdom and knowledge, there came a point when He knew with fulness who He was and what He had to accomplish. We do not know precisely when that full awareness occurred, but it surely preceded those special days of stress in the wilderness.[2]

Unsurprisingly, Satan appeared at this time of maximum importance for what he hoped would also be a time of maximum vulnerability: "Lo, he [the Lord] shall suffer temptations, and pain of body, hunger, thirst, and fatigue, even more than man can suffer."[3]

Perhaps this period of temptation was the most difficult of all for the Savior—except for those later hours in Gethsemane and on Calvary. The dawning of the enormity of what He had yet to do; the weight and fate of so many souls resting upon Him; the realization that He, though innocent, must, in achieving the Atonement, experience the "fierceness" of the justice of God; and the reality that He could actually choose—or refuse—to go through with it all: No one has ever faced anything like that! Yet Jesus was not exempted from the challenge of temptations common to mankind. As Elder Bruce R. McConkie has written: "Jesus was tempted—if we may so say—to fulfill all righteousness. It was part of the eternal plan. It gave him the experiences he needed to work out his own salvation, and it prepared him to sit in judgment upon his erring brethren, who, in a lesser degree, are tried and tested as he was."[4]

Total obedience and submissiveness would be required; hence the Savior's prolonged fasting, subjecting His mortal body to His divine spirit.

Then Satan proposed to the hungry and weary Jesus the barbed challenge: "If thou be the Son of God, command these stones be made bread."[5] Ironically, this first temptation came from him who once declared that, if chosen as Savior, he would not lose "one soul";[6] now Satan sought to overturn the salvation of all souls! So much for Satan's integrity and sincerity.

In this first temptation, grim hunger combined with the possibility of doubting His identity. Was not the Creator of the world entitled to some food? Had He not fasted long enough? Should not Father give Him a sign and fresh affirmation of His identity? Would He not suffer enough later on to make unnecessary further suffering in that place of solitude? Though Jesus may have had *none* such thoughts, this first temptation was not abstract or imaginary but real, for in all His temptations, as Elder Talmage wrote, Jesus was peccable—capable of sin—but remained sinless.[7]

And so Satan strove, for if the wedge of doubt could be driven in now, how many more times and how much deeper later on? Especially on Golgotha, when the taunting "if" would be repeated—and at the apogee of Jesus' agony. If Jesus could not be sure now of His identity and mission, what about subsequent challenges, such as before Pilate when a few words of even mild disclaimer would surely have freed Him, for Pilate would find no fault with Him?

If Christ commanded the stones to be made bread now, why not, later on, command the legions of angels to rescue Him from the cross? If He let Himself feel forsaken now, could Christ "hold out" later on? If He used His power for personal gratification now, why not later on when, by using it, He could do so much good and for so many others?

Our puny minds can only infer, and it is very low-level inferring at that, the actual content of the drama that took place.

Count on Satan, however, to know what questions to

put. In a moment of unimaginable hunger and of possible doubt of the Father and of self, the adversary, diabolically, did not select lesser temptations. Lucifer went for the jugular!

So it is with us. Our temptations, small or large, seem to match the moment. The evil one also avoids that which is most apt to be deflected by us.

Unlike our Lord, however, do we not justify a little self-indulgence occasionally in order to reward ourselves for being good? Understandably, do we not sometimes seek for added reassurance from Father—when we are amid personal stress and strain—or for a detour when the only way to go is through? Often in life, there is no "around." Do not we, too, know what it is to encounter divine restraint? God provides enough, but not all that we might like, by way of reassurance; there is sufficient "grace," but nothing extra.[8]

This first episode involving Jesus' temptations is one from which we can derive not only encouragement and insight about what to avoid but also how to dispatch temptation. Yet the realness of what tempts us, encountering it at a time of maximum personal vulnerability, the adversary's admixture of doubt and appetite, and pervasive self-pity— all of these can so easily converge in a way that causes us to demand that the Father make a showing of His watchcare for us. After all, up to now have we not done reasonably well for Him?

However, as our model in all things, what did the Master do? He gave a definitive response to the first temptation with no equivocation: "It is written, Man shall not live by bread alone, but by every word that proceedeth out of the mouth of God."[9] Jesus did not reprocess the temptation again and again.

Jehovah remained true to what He had said so many centuries before.[10] Though Moses, a marvelous prophet, once briefly arrogated power to himself, this Jesus resolutely refused to do!

Had Jesus not (in this circumstance of solitude and aloneness) been true to Himself and His trust, could He centuries later have justifiably urged Joseph Smith and the saints of this dispensation as follows? "For you shall live by every word that proceedeth forth from the mouth of God."[11] Jesus' integrity was at stake, and He prevailed. By being subject to temptation, He knew firsthand, "according to the flesh," how to succor us in our temptations—as well as how to extend divine *mercy* when, unlike Him, we succumb.

The Lord has declared not only of this first temptation, but of all His genuine and varied temptations, that He "gave no heed unto them." Yet He was tempted, not representatively, but "in all points." Once put, however, Jesus dismissed each of these summarily. He did not temporize with temptations. He "yielded not."[12] And neither should we.

Brooding over temptations can produce self-pity and a false sense of nobility. Prolonged consideration of a temptation only increases the risks—but it does not increase our options: the two options and the consequences remain the same regardless of our dallying.

Moreover, protracted consideration of a temptation does not increase the justification to succumb—only our rationalization. When we are well taught, we know, initially, what must be done. Therefore, to give heed to temptation is, in effect, to "give place" for Satan's seed to grow and sprout and to bring forth its bitter harvest.

So it was that Jesus, for the first recorded time, met the

awful *if*. It was a word to be repeated later when the stress
was even greater.[13] So we should do likewise. Otherwise,
to host an *if* is like hosting an insect that breeds and multi-
plies in the sun of circumstance. Soon one is crawling with
ifs and is thereby overcome. Some doubters who are overcome even become proud of their doubts—rather like being
proud of one's humility!

Just as quickly as Jesus thus dispatched the *first* temptation, there came a *second*. This follow-on episode, too, con-
tains lessons for us. Even past victories can subtly make us
vulnerable if we are not careful. It was Paul who warned:
"Wherefore let him that thinketh he standeth take heed lest
he fall."[14]

The second temptation reiterated the *if*: Satan urged
Jesus to cast Himself from the pinnacle of the temple to
bring about a demonstration of the Father's divine protec-
tion. The adversary even cleverly quoted scripture,
suggesting that Jesus would be spared and watched over.[15]
Jesus' scriptural rejoinder was immediate: "Jesus said unto
him, It is written again, Thou shalt not tempt the Lord thy
God." All this, too, foreshadowed a later temptation.[16]

So far as our salvation is concerned, immediacy in re-
jecting temptation has everything to commend it. Lucifer is
best dispatched at the doorstep—not after he's been invited in and has unpacked his things.

A lesser soul than Jesus could have surely rationalized
receiving some divine aid at this critical juncture. Would
not an impressive miracle help the work? Elder Talmage as-
serted, in this second temptation, that Satan was actually
tempting Jesus to tempt the Father. Did not Lucifer have a
long-standing grievance with Father? Was it not bound up
in that moment when the Father said, "I will send the
first"?[17] This later drama atop Father's house was but an ex-
tension of an earlier drama in our Father's premortal

household. This later confrontation and temptation concerning identity and misuse of power was soon over, however.

The focus shifted in the *third* temptation. The Spirit took
Jesus to a mountaintop, and there came the offer that could
not be refused. Yet it was!

"Again, the devil . . . sheweth him all the kingdoms of
the world, and the glory of them; and saith unto him, All
these things will I give thee, if thou wilt fall down and worship me."[18]

Luke provides some amplification: "And the devil said
unto him, *All this power will I give thee, and the glory of them:*
for that is delivered unto me; and to whomsoever I will I
give it. If thou therefore wilt *worship me, all shall be thine.*"[19]

From atop the Mount of Temptation, Jesus declared:
"Get thee hence, Satan: for it is written, Thou shalt worship
the Lord thy God, and him only shalt thou serve."[20]

Perhaps the adversary hoped Jesus would actually consider a mortal Messiahship in which He could commence
His reign at once. Perhaps the adversary hoped Jesus
would reflect on how, by so doing, He could accomplish so
much good, fulfilling the very type of Messiahship that, by
the way, the Jews were confidently expecting.

Satan obviously hoped Jesus would take second place,
so Satan could have that preeminence once refused him.
The rebel made his new bid for ascendancy, but, again, he
was dispatched!

As soon as these three major temptations were over,
angels came to minister to Jesus. But Jesus, hearing that
His beloved John the Baptist was in jail, dispatched angels
to minister instead unto the latter.[21] Does not this act of
matchless selflessness and empathy tell us much about the
divine nature of our Lord?

A defeated Satan departed from Jesus, but only for a

season. Remember, Lucifer is an incurable insomniac. But Jesus had won an enormous victory!

What further lessons emerge for us from the temptations of Jesus?

Just as personal goodness in mortality consists of accumulating service rather than a single act, so temptation is not a one-time thing either. The points of our personal vulnerability, as Satan cunningly observes them, will be exploited. Lucifer will quote scripture if it helps, or cite supposed opportunities for us to do good. He will offer chances for self-indulgence and even provide the preparatory self-pity—whatever might induce rationalization on our part.

Therefore, our challenge is to do as Jesus did—first, to resist temptation by giving it "no heed."

Our doubts will also be used against us. Equivalent *ifs* will be flung at us, like satanic darts designed to inflict pain. Circumstances may be used to cause us to call into question our true identity and our past spiritual knowledge. In fact, is not apostasy a denial of that which was once genuinely known but which now comes to be doubted, discounted, and discarded? Neglected and unnourished, the tree of testimony is, alas, plucked up and cast out.[22] But the tree was there, a fact to which its dried branches and roots are stark witness.

Power and authority and position, as Jesus taught and showed us, are not to be misused by us for personal gain or self-gratification. Almost all—not just a few—succumb to this particular temptation. Jesus was the enormous exception.[23] Gloriously, Jesus did not succumb. Our opportunities to do selflessly likewise will occur more than once in our lives, and we are much more likely to do likewise if we are meek and humble.

Temptations continue with us as with Jesus to the end, and past victories should not cause us to be casual or over-confident. Later, Jesus even thanked the Twelve for accompanying Him, saying, "Ye are they which have continued with me in my temptations."[24]

We can help each other in times of temptation as well as trial. We genuinely need, as John prescribed, the supportive fellowship of those who walk in the light.[25] What's *ahead* is made more clear only as the adversary is put *behind* us. Lucifer clouds not only our view of the present but also our perception of the future.

We know the tempter will be completely bound in the Millennium—but we can surely constrain him much sooner, so far as our lives are concerned: "Yea, verily, verily I say unto you, if all men had been, and were, and ever would be, like unto Moroni, behold, the very powers of hell would have been shaken forever; yea, the devil would *never have power* over the hearts of the children of men."[26]

In major episodes involving Jesus such as these three temptations, there are great truths to be savored!

Such is also the case in the less pondered episodes of the Master's life as, having reviewed Jesus' pattern of avoidance of evil deeds, we now examine His example in affirmation by good deeds.

Noteworthy, for instance, is how Christ met head-on false entreaties and praise that so often entrap us. "Jesus answered him, Sayest thou this thing of thyself, or did others tell it thee of me?"[27] No one is more loving of men and yet more unsusceptible to the praise and flattery of men than Jesus.

He was also, on occasion, understandably wistful. Once He asked aloud, in what must have been more of a lamentation than a question, if, when the Son of Man came again (in the Second Coming), would He "find faith on the earth."[28] Even this lamentation is a reflection of His deep love even for the faithless, and yet it is a recognition of the role and toll of free agency.

He knew and knows the bearing capacity of His disciples. Having taught the American disciples on one occasion, He then told them to go to their homes and discuss what He had taught them in their families and to prepare their minds for the morrow.[29] Not only milk before meat, but even the milk was given gradually.

Being the perfect Teacher, Jesus knew the value of silence. He could have said so much, but He nevertheless chose, standing before certain of His accusers prior to His crucifixion, to answer nothing. He also knew, as we must come to know, likewise, the value of some solitude: "And when he had sent the multitudes away, he went up into a mountain apart to pray: and when the evening was come, he was there alone."[30]

He who was reviled reviled not in return. And, to be like Him, we must do likewise. "Be patient in afflictions, revile not against those that revile. Govern your house in meekness, and be steadfast."[31]

Jesus discerned deep down goodness. Rather than let the impending but temporary skepticism in Thomas control all else, He called Thomas. Did not that insightful and brave apostle say, "Let us also go, that we might die with him"?[32] Jesus knows the sheep of His fold not only for *what they now are* but also for *what they have the power to become*.

We are sometimes so quick to classify and to stereotype. The Nazarenes rejected Jesus because He was the carpenter's son. But, ironically, Nazareth enjoyed no great prestige for itself, for did not Nathanael (in whom Jesus said there was no guile) ask, "Can there any good thing come out of Nazareth?" Discerning Jesus saw possibilities in Nathanael despite the latter's susceptibility to mild stereotyping, and promised the believing Nathanael, "Hereafter ye shall see heaven open, and the angels of God ascending and descending upon the Son of Man."[33]

Can we not do likewise and forgo some of our provincialism even when it arises out of the provincialism of others?

Furthermore, in Jesus, all the marvelous and eternal attributes are kept in a splendid symmetrical balance such as we observe concerning the woman taken in adultery. She went uncondemned by Him, but she was not sent on her way without knowing that she had sinned seriously. Unlike today's "rehabilitators," Jesus did not indulge in demeaning and expiating explanations of why she wrongly did what she did. Rather, He helped her to face stern reality. He encouraged her: "Go, and sin no more."[34] Thus we witness interplay of Jesus' justice and mercy. Contrition was already present in the woman, as Jesus, through divine discernment, knew. Needing to be both corrected and reassured, there was, in His instructions, confirmation of her wrong but also assurance for her future. Nor did she seek to excuse herself on the grounds that she, as a victim of circumstances, was hopelessly locked into a pattern of living that simply could not be changed.

How different from the ways of the world in which some want to be excused from their sins because they were "made that way"! Can anyone seriously seek to instruct the Creator concerning how things are made?

While the gospel of Jesus Christ is the gospel of hope, it does not concur in the excuses of congenital, behavioral infirmities or in all-encompassing environmental excuses. What is mortal, conventional wisdom, compared to eternal standards? Was not each swine in the Gadarene herd following a clear and compelling trend? *Totus porcus!*

Strange as it is, there are those who deliberately cultivate a sense of fundamental hopelessness and who therein seek to justify, to cover, and to continue in their sins. Just as too much physical idleness can induce lust, so intellectual slackness provides the dusk in which wrong deeds are considered, rationalized, and then encouraged.

Fittingly, the lasting marks of Jesus' truths and traits are to be seen in the personalities of those who truly strive to do likewise. For instance, his selflessness and His warnings about being too concerned with this world's goods found their way into the life patterns among members of the Church in the meridian day:

"And the multitude of them that believed were of one heart and of one soul: neither said any of them that ought of the things which he possessed was his own; but they had all things common. And with great power gave the apostles witness of the resurrection of the Lord Jesus: and great grace was upon them all."[35]

One also sees in the experiences of the Twelve, led by Peter, how they began to manage the burgeoning Church according to that which had been taught them by the Master, as in the episode concerning the welfare needs of certain Greek widows. Qualified individuals were called to minister to the needs of the widows in order that the Twelve could continue with their ministry, for, they said, "It is not reason that we should leave the word of God, and serve tables."[36]

The Twelve could easily but wrongly have contained their ministry to Jerusalem, becoming regional welfare administrators. They would surely have been busy, and the people there would have loved them for their personal attentiveness. But such was not their calling. Having been tutored and trained by the Savior, they increased in wisdom and stature. "And the word of God increased; and the number of the disciples multiplied in Jerusalem greatly; and a great company of the priests were obedient to the faith."[37] Thanks to a wise decision, the Church grew, but not just in Jerusalem!

One has only to read the powerful answer of Stephen, the martyr, to his accusers to see how Jesus' widening circle of influence encompassed still others.

Stephen had been brought before the council by a false witness on a false charge of blasphemy, "words against Moses, and against God." Stephen had not said words *against* Moses or Jehovah but *for* them. In many ways, Stephen was prepared all of his life (though not solely) for the moment when he would be called upon to respond to his accusers, and he rose to impressive spiritual heights, for his words are deeply touching as one reads and rereads them.

Following his "testimony of Jesus Christ," as Stephen was being slain, he behaved with mercy reminiscent of Jesus', of whom he had just given powerful testimony: "Lord, lay not this sin to their charge."[38]

Significantly, Stephen's testimony consisted not only of the fact that Jesus had been resurrected, but included implications that sent the Jewish hierarchy into a frenzy: Jesus was the sacred Jehovah and the expected Messiah! Stephen's testimony of seeing the Father with Jesus beside Him brought martyrdom. The establishment in our time is equally scornful of, and unnerved by, Joseph Smith's vision in which he, too, saw the Father with the Son at His side. Again, martyrdom followed.

Modern prophets in our day, like the Galilean fishermen, utter truths that many people are not able to bear. The establishment in the meridian of time was not threatened by the exalted Beatitudes of Jesus, but by the direct and clear testimonies of the exalted role of Jesus of Nazareth. Sufficient unto each dispensation are the stumbling blocks thereof!

This matter of how divine disclosure matches people's readiness to receive is seen in yet another example. Not even a hundredth part of the things which Jesus did truly teach is recorded in the Book of Mormon. The things written there represent "a lesser part of the things which he taught the people." Why is this so? The lesser part is provided, said Jesus, "to try their faith"—to see how much receptivity there would be. Mormon wanted to "write . . . all which were engraven upon the plates of Nephi, but the Lord forbade it, saying: I will try the faith of my people."[39]

Given full divine awareness of the human tendency to stumble needlessly, the above scriptures are sobering. How vital the attributes of humility and meekness in this mortal proving process!

Stumbling over the scriptures (as did the Jews who would not pay heed to Jesus because He was from Galilee, whereas the Messiah was to be born in Bethlehem) is an attitude that did not end in the meridian of time. So many have since interpreted the words of John the Apostle as indicating there would be no more prophets and revelations.[40] Likewise, the very appearance of the words "The End of the Prophets" after the book of Malachi in the King James Version of the Bible has created a similar block for many. Hence the need for us all to be childlike in both our receptivity to additional revelations and our willingness to walk to the edge of available light before expecting more light.

Not only was Jesus fully and perfectly aware of the prophecies of the Old Testament that bore upon His earthly ministry—so, to a lesser degree, were His apostles. When Paul wrote about how Jesus was to the Jews a stumbling block, was he not merely echoing what another prophet, Isaiah, had foretold so many centuries before? "And he shall be a sanctuary; but for a stone of stumbling and for a rock of offence to both the houses of Israel, for a gin and for a snare to the inhabitants of Jerusalem."[41]

No doubt someday we shall see that the gradations of disclosure had to be so, perhaps in part as an act of mercy, lessening the condemnation of those who would have rejected the more part had they received even more.

In pondering the fearlessness of the Master during His mortal ministry, it is altogether too easy to ascribe His courage to the fact that He would have been protected from any physical harm by angelic protectors if necessary. Jesus' fearlessness rested upon His righteousness; therein lay His sole security. The powers of heaven were His only insofar as He remained as He did—righteous. It is the same with us.

But there are much more subtle forms of fear, as we all know. We sometimes fear what people will think *of* us more than what they will do *to* us. For instance, had Jesus been less filled with integrity than He was, He could have shaded the truth just a bit, hoping to curry the favor (or at least the neutrality) of those in power.

If He was not truly meek, Jesus could have put on more convincing displays of His power, hoping to increase His following. If He were less than our Lord He could have basked in more adulation, had He merely issued less stinging criticism of things as they then were.

But there was divine determination in Him to do what

He had been asked to do, and to do it fearlessly. He was not afraid of being misunderstood. He was not afraid of being alone, though right. He was not afraid that all that He did would then, and in the centuries to come, go largely unrecognized. He was not afraid to ordain the Twelve, imperfect as they were, because He knew both them and the Source of their guidance. Though we cannot even approach His fearlessness, we can begin to do likewise by subduing our fears of men.

Christ's refusal to entertain these and other fears and his dispatching of them, permits us to view, in some small measure, His marvelous courage. Obviously, the eternal attributes are interactive, but courage calls the cadence for summoning these attributes into action.

Jesus' fearlessness, however, was accompanied by gentleness. When He healed ten lepers and only one returned to thank Him, He then asked, "But where are the nine?"[42] There was no point in His lecturing the one—as we so often do, giving the right lesson to the wrong audience—instead of the other nine. After all, the one did return!

There for us to ponder is the often neglected but insightful second sermon of Jesus in the synagogue at Nazareth from which He earlier had been thrust out and threatened with death.[43] We see His mercy in this provision of an added opportunity for those in the hometown of His youth; it was His "own country." This time, however, listeners were astonished instead of enraged. What happened next, however, is both illuminating and discouraging: He was rejected not because of *what* He said or *how* He said it—rather, because of *who* He was perceived to be: "Is not this the carpenter, the son of Mary?" Then came Jesus' well-known lamentation: "A prophet is not without honour, but in his own country, and among his own kin, and in his own house."[44]

In short, "they were offended at him." No spiritual work, save the healing of a few sick folk, could be done. Then it was recorded of Jesus, who had seen so much disbelief at Nazareth, that "he marvelled because of their unbelief." Think upon it! They were His neighbors and had some awareness of at least some of His mighty works—yet all this was dismissed because He was a local individual. Often that which we, too, can do is so limited by the agency and the stereotyping of others.

May it also be that a whole people can likewise be airily dismissed, even resented, by their contemporaries and fellow citizens for the same reasons? Yes!

One wonders if the reaction to Jesus' first visit to Nazareth—rage—was not in some respects preferable to the deliberate disdain experienced in connection with his second visit. Satan's stratagems are apparent: If one cannot face truth, then he can merely dismiss it by stereotyping the source. Dismiss the message because of the lowly messengers.

A corollary to the above incident is found in the words of Moroni, who affirmed the "many mighty miracles" of Jesus. Moroni declared that if miracles dwindled among the children of men, it would be because of their unbelief. But why the unbelief? Because, said Moroni, people *"know not the God* in whom they should trust." Exactly the point Jesus made in the episode with the Samaritan woman!⁴⁵

It causes some pondering when one notes that unbelief may be connected to the failure of many to understand the nature of God. For the humble, knowing accurately what God is like facilitates genuine belief. But vagueness about God soon sours into disbelief, and when *believing* ceases, so, usually, does the *doing*. Likewise do the miracles.

What the Twelve heard Jesus speak about in the parable of the unprofitable servant provides another needed insight about doing.[46] As with certain of His other utterances, this commentary seems harsh at first. Why should one be thanked merely for doing his duty? Why should not the weary servant see first to the needs of his master? Servants come second, and so on. Of course, apostolic obedience was being taught as well as the leader-servant posture.

But more was also being taught: God's generosity toward us is not to be expressed by the dilution of the demands of duty that He lays upon us. Where much is given, much is expected—not the other way around. Nor is divine generosity to be expressed by a lessening of God's standards concerning what is to be done. Rather, when much is given and much is done by the disciple, then God's generosity is overwhelming!

When we have given and done our all, we will one day receive "all that [our] Father hath."[47] Therein lies God's generosity. When we do our duty, He is bound—and gladly bound. Being perfect in His love, He desires to reward us as befits a Perfect Father. Therefore, His generosity to His servants comes in the ratio of blessings given to duty done—but *not* in a slackening of His standards or in duties diminished. As we think upon it, would we really want it any other way? Kindness never takes the form of permissiveness!

Moreover, God's mercy and generosity have to do with what happens as we fail, not with insuring the absence of failures simply because the demands made were too light. Besides, how could there be real sanctification without real consecration?

Our comparative unprofitability in the parable cited is further explained by the lesser significance of what we accomplish even as doers, when that is placed beside what

Jesus has done. Even so, how redemptive and filled with mercy Jesus is as we are given continuous opportunities to overcome our imperfections.

In contrast to Jesus' merciful redemptiveness, the adversary's approach focuses on Peter's lapse in the hall of the high priest, rather than on Peter's bold and ringing affirmation before the council.[48] By playing upon the weaknesses of men, the adversary can easily persuade many that these weaknesses are so congenital that they cannot (indeed, need not) be overcome. However, the message merciful Jesus has given us clearly confirms that while our weaknesses are unmistakably there, if, like little children, we will follow Him, doing "likewise," we too can overcome and mature just as did Peter.

Embedded in this warming reality is the resplendent truth that with all of our imperfections, if we are humble and meek, we too can be used by Him. The fact that the perfect Lord works through imperfect people should not obscure the divinity of the callings that come to imperfect people, any more than people could rightly disregard John the Baptist's warning counsel simply because they did not approve of his rugged diet—or dismiss the doctrines of these plain Galileans merely because they were only fishermen.

The adversary would be pleased to have us focus on Paul's and Peter's differences over a particular, but passing, policy of the Church in the meridian of time. Though real, these differences do not tell us about the richness in the relationship of Peter and Paul in which they pursued their special brotherhood of the apostolic calling, proclaiming whithersoever they went—even unto death—their witness that Jesus lived, lives, and would come again!

To focus on Peter's failure to continue to walk on water ignores the fact that, for a few brief moments, he was a part of a genuine and unrivaled miracle. Though briefly, he actually walked with Jesus—whose special witness he was. What other mortal has done likewise?

Furthermore, even when leaders display imperfection, the spiritual sophistication with which those imperfections should be viewed is displayed for us by a marvelous and meek prophet, Moroni, who said: "Condemn me not because of mine imperfection, neither my father, because of his imperfection, neither them who have written before him; but rather give thanks unto God that he hath made manifest unto you our imperfections, that ye may learn to be more wise than we have been."[49]

In a true disciple, no one regrets a lapse more than the sincere lapser.

Who more than writers of God's word, themselves, are as conscious of the imperfections in their writings? Moroni, for instance, wrote: "And whoso receiveth this record, and shall not condemn it because of the imperfections which are in it, the same shall know of greater things than these. Behold, I am Moroni; and were it possible, I would make all things known unto you."[50]

And who, more than the Lord, knows what processing His truths through weak mortals costs? "Behold, I am God and have spoken it; these commandments are of me, and were given unto my servants in their weakness, after the manner of their language, that they might come to understanding."[51] Moreover, we should never use the imperfections of another as an excuse not to address our own imperfections.

The episode involving Thomas B. Marsh is very instructive. He let a dispute over milk cause him to focus, jealously rather than mercifully, on some minor imperfections in the Prophet Joseph Smith, which finally led to the excommunication of Brother Marsh. Lorenzo Snow, Thomas Marsh's contemporary, said that while he, too, noticed some minor imperfections in the Prophet, he was grateful that the Lord could use Joseph Smith for so very significant a work. Thus, there might be some hope for him, Lorenzo Snow. Indeed, here was hope for President Snow, who viewed others graciously and charitably as if through the "windows of heaven."

Another example is Aaron, who, though he erred significantly, still has one of the Holy Priesthoods named after him, and his calling by a prophet is still cited as a model. How generous and merciful is our God! It is interesting to read how each time Aaron erred, a loving and meek Moses mediated for him and prayed for him, reflecting the growing compassion and mercy Moses had. Now Aaron has the veneration of generations, for the Lord tutored him and magnified him.

Father Lehi joined briefly in murmuring when things got exceedingly difficult, but he soon hearkened to the Lord after being chastened because of his murmurings. Has not the Lord told us, "whom the Lord loveth, He chasteneth"?[52]

The tutoring of Joseph Smith "in [his] weakness" continued until the very end. Later this accolade was given: "Joseph Smith, the Prophet and Seer of the Lord, has done more, save Jesus only, for the salvation of men in this world, than any other man that ever lived in it."[53]

In studying Jesus' brief post-resurrection ministry among the Nephites, it is instructive to ponder the precious things He did within the precious time allotted. These clearly showed His priorities and tell us much about what we are to do, including the avoidance of those things which could obscure the "simpleness of the way."[54]

Christ presented Himself as witness to His own resurrection; He let the multitude feel and see His wounds; He testified of Himself; He instituted the ordinance of baptism. He established an apostolic priesthood organization through the calling of the Nephite Twelve; He gave much attention on how to pray, teaching His followers, almost clinically, how to pray, using His Twelve Apostles and dividing the people into twelve groups.

Significantly, as those disciples were attuned to the Spirit when in the posture and attitude of prayer, they were actually given what they should pray about: "And it came to pass that when Jesus had thus prayed unto the Father, he came unto his disciples, and behold, they did still continue, without ceasing, to pray unto him; and they did not multiply many words, for it was given unto them what they should pray, and they were filled with desire."[55]

He taught the multitude concerning the sacrament. He ensured that the Gift of the Holy Ghost was bestowed upon the faithful. He blessed their children. He taught them about yet other sheep whom He was to visit.

He took time to instruct the Twelve. He commended the people for their faith. He entrusted to them a more complete understanding concerning the Gentiles. He gave them the Sermon on the Mount and the Sermon on the Plain. He urged and instructed them to search the scriptures, and expounded the scriptures to them. He reproved them for omissions in their own records. He rehearsed to them Malachi's words. He gave a description of the final judgment within which, significantly, some of the divine attributes are cited: "If they be good, to the resurrection of everlasting life; and if they be evil, to the resurrection of damnation; being on a parallel, the one on the one hand and the other on the other hand, according to the mercy, and the justice, and the holiness which is in Christ, who was before the world began."[56]

He gave them clear instructions concerning the name of the Church and prevented disputations among them by giving them certain other instructions. As we see the Savior's simple directness, no wonder Paul wrote of the "simplicity that is in Christ."[57]

For those of us who desire to contemplate our own ministry in the instructive context of what Jesus did in those special days, the above recitation is illuminating. But it is also sobering in its focus on fundamentals and in its simplicity. Remember, in our own ministry, we are to do "likewise." How simplicity adds to felicity! How complications can add to our vexations!

Our joy depends upon the degree to which we are like Him and serve as He did, even amid trial. Are we not advised that glory comes only after tribulation? "For after much tribulation come the blessings. Wherefore the day cometh that ye shall be crowned with much glory; the hour is not yet, but is nigh at hand."[58]

Our only true peace really consists of that inner peace which comes from keeping His commandments and the assurances He has given us. In this world we are to have tribulation. Even so, He said, "Be of good cheer; I have overcome the world."[59] For the faithful, there is short-term tribulation but long-term joy.

Temptation and trial are part of our toughening tutorials—the only toughening, by the way, that is also a sweetening. Even with all these reassurances, however, will we not feel, on occasion, as though—with so many deeds to be done—we are being overwhelmed? Undoubtedly. We may also feel that our particular assemblage of affliction is perhaps larger than that of anyone else. Nephi recorded this indicator of how he once felt: "And it came to pass that I was overcome because of my afflictions, for I considered that *mine afflictions were great above all*, because of the destruction of my people, for I had beheld their fall."[60]

Nephi's capacity to lament genuinely over the wickedness of his colleagues is a reflection of His highly developed love for his associates and fellowmen. It was likewise with Enoch: "And as Enoch saw this, he had bitterness of soul, and wept over his brethren, and said unto the heavens: I will refuse to be comforted; but the Lord said unto Enoch: Lift up your heart, and be glad; and look."[61]

Even in the midst of Enoch's "bitterness of soul" because of the wickedness of his brethren and their fate, he was told to "be glad; and look." What did he see which brought comfort? He saw the Son of Man coming "in the meridian of time" to effect the Atonement! Thus, time and time again, we learn that the objective reality over which we are to be of good cheer consists of those fundamental and basic blessings, such as the unmatched Atonement, that are irrevocably in place. The disappointments of the day must not obscure the basic blessings of eternity!

So much of our capacity to do "likewise" rests on our trust in God's timing, since His love for us is not at issue. To question His timing is a tacit questioning of His perfect love and knowledge. Moreover, part of our meekness, as we strive to do as He did, consists of trusting the Lord for placing us upon the earth at a particular time. Wishing to have lived in another time will not do as a substitute for performing in our own time, as Nephi, the son of Helaman, lamented: "Oh *that I could have had my days in the days when my father Nephi first came out of the land of Jerusalem*, that I could have joyed with him in the promised land; then were his people easy to be entreated, firm to keep the commandments of God, and slow to be led to do iniquity; and they were quick to hearken unto the words of the Lord— Yea, *if my days could have been in those days,* then would my soul have had joy in the righteousness of my brethren. But behold, I am *consigned that these are my days,* and that my soul shall be filled with sorrow because of this the wickedness of my brethren."[62]

In this respect, Jesus gave us a needed lesson about timing. Did He not send forth the Twelve instructing them not to go "into the way of the Gentiles, and into any city of the Samaritans"? Why? Because they were rather to go "to the lost sheep of the house of Israel."[63] Did not Jesus for a moment withhold a healing from the daughter of a woman of Canaan? Though He enunciated that He had been sent only to the lost sheep of the house of Israel, He made an exception in the case of this woman because of her faith, and her daughter was "made whole from that very hour."[64]

Just how long it was from the time of divine constraint regarding sharing the gospel with the Gentiles until Peter and others received the marvelous divine instructions to take the gospel to them, we do not know precisely. But it did involve some time.

The issue for us is trusting God enough to trust also His timing. If we can truly believe He has our welfare at heart, may we not let His plans unfold as He thinks best? The same is true with the second coming and with all those matters wherein our faith needs to include faith in the Lord's timing for us personally, not just in His overall plans and purposes.

We see this willingness of the Lord to wait upon our readiness in yet another episode: his conversation with two disciples on the road to Emmaus. As Jesus joined them in the conversation, they did not know Him. Why did He not simply announce who He was, declaring in testimony His identity? Only later, as they invited Him as a guest in their house, were "their eyes opened, and they knew him; and he vanished out of their sight."[65]

Embedded deep within these episodes is the almost overwhelming realization of the elaborate and personalized pains to which the Master goes in order to teach us when we are ready—but then with a thoroughness that makes the lesson everlasting.

Insights are embedded in even the smallest of episodes concerning which we are blessed to have a record. For instance, there is Jesus' declaration to Jeremiah: "Before I formed thee in the belly I knew thee; and before thou camest forth out of the womb I sanctified thee, and I ordained thee a prophet unto the nations."[66] We do not know precisely why Jesus told Jeremiah this. Perhaps Jeremiah needed some reassuring and reinforcing. But it stands as a pointed lesson for us all as to God's long-range planning and the inevitable role played by timing—and not just for His prophets! "To wait upon the Lord" carries several connotations for us all.

Yet this last episode does tell us something of Jesus' tutorial relationships with His prophets. Not only were these men foreordained by Him before they came to this life, but He also foresaw their adequacy to perform the mortal labors for which they had been previously set apart, an enormously important message for us all to ponder.

In addition, we learn that Jesus always honors those who honor Him. As we see Shadrach, Meschach, and Abednego in the midst of the fiery furnace, it is significant that walking among them as they were there unharmed was one in form "like the Son of God."[67] Whether it is Paul in prison or three valiant young men taking a stand against a secularized king, the Lord is near at hand in our hour of greatest need—sometimes dramatically, sometimes quietly.

Our loyalty to principle in the midst of our fiery trials and to particular persons is yet another way of our doing "likewise."

And if we need any further verification about the significance of being meek and childlike, so far as qualifying for the Kingdom of God is concerned, it is seen in the readiness of children to receive revelations even greater than those given to some adults:

"And it came to pass that he did teach and minister unto the children of the multitude of whom hath been spoken, and he did loose their tongues, and they did speak unto their fathers great and marvelous things, *even greater than he had revealed unto the people;* and he loosed their tongues that they could utter."[68]

Childlike faith in the need to "do likewise" is especially vital when, in our pseudosophistication, we rationalize that the deed to be done may not really matter after all, so why bother? It matters—and more than we know. To be submissive "even as a child doth submit to his Father" is a hard saying, but it is more than poetry; it reminds us of our true genealogy and our true possibility.

Among the resurrected Jesus' last recorded words to the people whom He taught in the Americas were words especially encouraging to emulators. To the Three Nephites Christ described what lay ahead of them; then, significantly, He promised that each, if faithful, would "sit down in the kingdom" of the Father. "Yea, your joy shall be full," He declared, "even as the Father hath given me fulness of joy; and ye shall be *even as I am*, and I am even as the Father; and the Father and I are one."[69]

Since Jesus urges us to become even as He is, this bold but tender indication to these three individuals assumes staggering significance. For the promise was given not alone to them but to all the faithful. That such could happen at all should fill us with gratitude and wonder. These closing words of Christ are words that give special hope for the doers of His word.

Footnotes

[1]Luke 10:37.
[2]Talmage, *Jesus the Christ*, p. 128. See also Luke 20:44; D&C 93:11-14.
[3]Mosiah 3:7.
[4]McConkie, *The Mortal Messiah* 1:417.
[5]Matthew 4:3.
[6]Moses 4:1.
[7]Talmage, *Jesus the Christ*, pp. 134-35.
[8]2 Corinthians 12:9; Ether 12:26.
[9]Matthew 4:4.
[10]Deuteronomy 8:3.
[11]D&C 84:44.
[12]D&C 20:22. See also Hebrews 2:18; 4:14-15.
[13]See Luke 23:35-39.
[14]1 Corinthians 10:23. See also D&C 58:15.
[15]Psalm 91:11-12.
[16]Matthew 4:7; 27:40. See also Deuteronomy 6:16.
[17]Abraham 3:37.
[18]Matthew 4:8-9.
[19]Luke 4:6-7. Italics added.
[20]Matthew 4:10.
[21]JST Matthew 4:11.
[22]See Alma 32:38-39.
[23]See D&C 121:39.
[24]Luke 22:28.
[25]1 John 1:6-7.
[26]Alma 48:17. Italics added.
[27]John 18:34.
[28]Luke 18:8.
[29]3 Nephi 17:3.
[30]Matthew 27:12; 14:23.
[31]D&C 31:9.
[32]John 11:16.
[33]John 1:46-47, 51.
[34]John 8:3-11.

[35]Acts 4:32-33. See also Moses 7:18.

[36]Acts 6:2.

[37]Acts 6:7.

[38]Acts 6 and 7. We usually think of balancing our discipleship in words and deeds by stressing more *doing* and less *talking*. We are to be "doers of the word," lest we be hypocrites. Spiritual symmetry requires, however, that "doers" also be willing to be declarative, as was valiant Stephen. The "how" of their religious life is in clear and happy evidence. But it would strengthen some to hear more of the "what" and "why" that produce such Christian living. Some followers do not make the aforementioned linkage clear, leaving those who are weak in the faith with unnecessary doubts. Understating the faith is not always, therefore, a matter of deficiency in deeds, but sometimes consists of the follower's failure to open his mouth because of the fear of men. (See D&C 60:2.) Stephen's deeds and declaratives were classically matched.

[39]3 Nephi 26:6-11.

[40]Revelation 22:18-19.

[41]Isaiah 8:14.

[42]Luke 17:17.

[43]Luke 4:28-30.

[44]Mark 6:1-6.

[45]Mormon 9:18-20; John 4:22. Italics added.

[46]Luke 17:7-10.

[47]D&C 84:38.

[48]Luke 22:54-62; Acts 4:5-12.

[49]Mormon 9:31.

[50]Mormon 8:12.

[51]D&C 1:24.

[52]1 Nephi 19:20; Hebrews 12:6.

[53]D&C 35:17; 124:1; 135:3.

[54]1 Nephi 17:41.

[55]3 Nephi 19:24.

[56]3 Nephi 26:5.

[57]2 Corinthians 11:3.

[58]D&C 58:4.

[59]John 16:33.

[60]1 Nephi 15:5. Italics added.

[61]Moses 7:44-46.

[62]Helaman 7:7-9. Italics added.

[63]Matthew 10:5-6.

[64]Matthew 15:21-28.

[65]Luke 24:13-31.

[66]Jeremiah 1:5.

[67]Daniel 3:25. See also D&C 38:7.

[68]3 Nephi 26:14. Italics added.

[69]3 Nephi 28:10. Italics added.

5

Be of Good Cheer

Jesus has repeatedly instructed us in yet another way in which we are to be like Him: We are to "be of good cheer."[1] Being of good cheer is the proximate preparation for ultimate joy. Being of good cheer—one day at a time—precedes that point later on when, if we live righteously, we can justifiably say what Jesus said: "Now behold, my joy is full."[2]

Gospel gladness is possible even in the midst of affliction, because of the reassuring realities that pertain to our mortal circumstance. The everlastingness of certain things puts the temporariness of other things in perspective. God's promises to us are so rich that even difficult tactical circumstances cannot conceal our causes for genuine cheerfulness: God is in charge; God's plan of happiness is underway; momentary tribulation does not set aside the universal resurrection, which is a reality; individual identity and personality are thereby assured; death has been defeated by Christ's atonement; and Satan and his misery-causing minions will finally be defeated. Each of these (and many more) form the litany of reassuring reality.

Thus we should not let the gray mists of the moment obscure the bright promises and prospects of eternity. Gospel gladness is a precious, precious perspective—essential to have, if one is to keep his attitudinal balance while traveling the straight and narrow way. The way is often no more than a path. It inclines sharply, and it is strewn with loose rocks. Indeed, there are points along the way to be traversed only on one's hands and knees.

As in all things, Jesus is also our attitudinal Exemplar as to cheerfulness.

When, just prior to the great intercessory prayer in Gethsemane, Jesus told Peter, James, and John to "be of good cheer," such an attitude was certainly not justified because of immediate circumstances. Instead, it was possible because Jesus had "overcome the world."[3] Contemplate, however, the grim experiences that then lay immediately ahead, scarcely justifying an attitude of cheerfulness. Gethsemane was imminent. So were Judas's betrayal; the capturing of Jesus, who was Peter, James, and John's beloved leader; Peter's disheartening disavowal; and Jesus' unjust trial. The populace's chilling preference for Barabbas rather than Jesus would soon echo in the air. The Shepherd would be smitten and the sheep scattered. Then there would be those awful, final moments on Calvary.

Therefore, what, pray tell, was there to be cheerful about? Yet in the face of all of this, Jesus told them to "be of good cheer"!

The glorious, irrevocable, and long-awaited Atonement was about to be accomplished. The adversary had failed to stop it. The resurrection was assured. Death was soon to be done away. Christ had overcome the world—not the reverse. These irrepressible realities, both then and now, give rise to gospel gladness, permitting us to be of good cheer even in the midst of tactical tribulation. True cheer is grounded in those signal triumphs but is also to be found in all the attendant developments.

Meanwhile, however, though our trials are tiny compared to His, alas, we are often grumpy. Jesus was of good cheer because then current conditions did not alter His sources of ultimate joy. Are not our fundamental sources of joy the same as His?

On still another occasion, Jesus used the same encouraging words when, having healed a paralytic, He did not emphasize the health restored; rather, He said, "Be of good cheer; thy sins be forgiven thee."[4] Like freedom from death, emancipation from error is always a special reason for being of good cheer.

When the Nephite members of the Church were virtual hostages and their lives were forfeit if the prophesied signs of Jesus' coming did not occur, yet they were told by the Lord to "be of good cheer." Why? Because on the morrow He would come into the world.[5] The first coming of the Savior, a milestone finally to be passed after centuries of expectant waiting, was at hand—yet another fundamental cause for rejoicing.

A failure on our part to achieve and sustain more than we do such a cheerful and precious perspective is yet another manifestation of the human tendency of "looking beyond the mark," of focusing on lesser things.

When Paul was in jail after having borne his testimony before a powerful political group in Jerusalem, Jesus stood by and counseled him to "be of good cheer."[6] Why? Had not Paul been struck on the mouth at Ananias's order? Were not forty Jews plotting his death? Did not his trial for sedition lie just ahead? And also Paul's shipwreck? Cheerfulness was possible because Paul had done well in his ministry in Jerusalem and now was ready for Rome, where he would also testify with great power and persuasive authority. Let the intervening, tactical tribulation come!

This lesson about justifiable cheerfulness even amid perilous passages apparently had been driven home to Paul, for during his voyage to Rome, he assured his fearful shipmates that not one of them would lose their lives, though their ship would be lost. Therefore, He encouraged them to "be of good cheer" in the midst of their anxieties, and his prophecy was fulfilled.[7]

It remains for us, therefore, to be of good cheer even when, as was the case with the original Twelve, current circumstances seem hopeless. In fact, seemingly sad circumstances may actually reflect *implementation*, not *disintegration*. Indeed, the unfolding of God's purposes may require the collapse of other things.

How often is it necessary for dismantling to occur in order for something better to be put in place? Was there ever a remodeling without distress and inconvenience? Was there ever fulfillment without certain things coming to an end? Moreover, the fundamental causes for such rejoicing and gospel gladness are clearly the same for us as for our predecessors.

It may seem to some of us so very hard to cling to those reassuring and renewing realities when tribulations and difficulties press in upon us from all sides. But these are the realities to which we will—and should—finally cling in the moments of truth. Why not, therefore, said Jesus, profit from good cheer at the outset and throughout each day, rather than finally relying upon it anyway—but only after unneeded anxiety?

Even when, momentarily, we lose our grip on gospel gladness, the Lord is long-suffering. We can regain lost perspective, favoring once again in our way of living that which is everlasting, not fleeting; the unending, not the momentary. By forgoing now, we can possess more later.

If we have a sense of proportion here and now, our portion hereafter will be significantly larger. Then, the mercy and love of God will provide for us such wondrous surroundings that "eye hath not seen" and "ear hath not heard" such things as the Lord will have prepared for us there. Has not He who is perfect in truth told us that in His Father's estate are *many* mansions—not a solitary mansion with a "No Vacancy" sign? Whatever it is that we righteously hope for here, if we are truly obedient it will be breathtakingly exceeded by what is given to us there.

The preciousness of gospel perspective may be thought of in still another way. Through the marvel of telecommunications in our time, we obtain satellite pictures of what we compositely call "the weather." We even see pictures of storm fronts moving in. Yet, just because we know a winter storm is coming, it is no less cold; the snow still falls with all of the attending and harsh consequences. But the overview permits us to know that the storm front, however severe, will pass away.

Likewise, the storm fronts that come into our lives will not last forever. We can surmount the drifts of difficulties and we can hold out if we maintain our perspective and faith. But while we are in the midst of all these things, the experiences that can be for our long-term good are very, very real. We may feel that such are simply more than we can bear. Yet if we have faith in an all-knowing and all-loving God, we understand He will not give us more than we can bear.[8]

Just as we know there is a sun just beyond today's cloud cover, so we must not doubt the continued, watchful, and tutoring presence of *The Son* in spite of the stormy seasons in our lives. Of such real, but transitory, things like the local weather, it might be said, "This too shall pass away," but of Jesus' words it is rightfully said that His "words shall not pass away."[9]

Jesus refused to be one of "woeful countenance." Not only did He refuse to let the establishment of the time tell Him with whom he might dine; He also refused to insist that people look mournful when they were fasting.[10] Though He was called "man of sorrows,"[11] that description refers to His bearing of *our* sorrows—not His; it does not describe His day-to-day bearing!

Indeed, given the overarching and resplendent realities, Jesus was able to teach His disciples to have a spirit of rejoicing about life. Hence we find Paul, who had known persecution and imprisonment, saying, "Rejoice in the Lord alway: and again I say, rejoice."[12] And why not? Had Paul not known rich and reassuring experiences? Can we not likewise take justifiable nourishment from our storehouse of memories—especially in stern seasons and in difficult days? Church members of another time did so in the face of an advancing army. Though fearful, they were reminded by a prophet that God could and would deliver them; this "hushed their fears."[13]

There is, however, one kind of pain and cheerlessness that Jesus would help us to avoid: suffering for our sins. He has told us that unless we repent (and oh, how He invites us to repent!), our suffering will be exquisite, for we must suffer even as He. Clearly, unrepentant individuals cannot now know good cheer.

Jesus even used the word *fierceness* to describe that justice of God which He would gladly spare us, if we would but repent.[14] Such suffering is whole-soul torment, not just the pain of body. He would surely spare us all of those forms of suffering and cheerlessness.

But as to other forms of pain that are common part and parcel of the human experience—from these there can be no full immunity. The cares of the world that, on occasion, can rob us of cheerfulness are certainly real cares, but they are not lasting cares; they pass with the passing of this world. Like the pleasures of the world, the cares of the world are fleeting.

Someday, when we look back on mortality, we will see that so many of the things that seemed to matter so much at the moment will be seen not to have mattered at all. And the eternal things will be seen to have mattered even more than the most faithful of the Saints imagined.

Furthermore, the attribute of being of good cheer is especially needed for those of us who are destined to live in a time of "wars and rumors of wars," when "peace shall be taken from the earth."[15]

Protracted war can seem to be ceaseless, especially to those who are intimately involved. This appears to have been the case in Book of Mormon times: "And no one knoweth the end of the war." In an even earlier period, we read these words—"And the wars ceased not."[16]

The anti-Christian overtones have been there, too: "For behold, their wars are exceedingly fierce among themselves; and because of their hatred they put to death every Nephite that will not deny the Christ."[17]

The trench warfare of World War I went on and on and on. Some participants thought they would never see its end. Close on the heels of World War I came the Spanish civil war, the Second World War, the Greek war, the Korean War, the Arab-Israeli wars, the Vietnam war, Afghanistan, and on and on it goes. Wars, large and small, seem to be the continuing experience of twentieth-century man.

Even so, the almost unceasingness of war is but the fulfilling echo of prophecy. Who knows better than the Lord that wars originate in the hearts and minds of man? In 1832 He revealed to Joseph Smith the coming American Civil War. A year earlier He had declared to the Prophet that Joseph knew not the hearts of his own countrymen.[18] Since then, there has been an almost unbroken chain of wars.

Can we presume to lecture the Lord on war? Or dare to use war as an argument against His existence or His Lordship? Do we need to warn Him about how the earth can be destroyed by fire?[19]

Those who have known what has been called the "strange, mournful mutter of the battlefield" carry that awful sound indelibly imprinted upon their memories. Such individuals can appreciate the paradoxical mix of the camaraderie and loneliness that goes with war. The warrior-prophet Moroni wrote in A.D. 401 about his father's death and said, "I even remain alone to write the sad tale of the destruction of my people." The sense of lamentation becomes even more profound a few lines later: "I am alone. My father hath been slain in battle, and all my kinsfolk, and I have not friends nor whither to go; and how long the Lord will suffer that I may live I know not."[20] Yet, though surrounded by *proximate* sadness, Moroni knew those *ultimate* reasons he had for being of good cheer. So it was that he testified of Christ and maintained his spiritual poise to the very end: "And now I bid unto all, farewell. I soon go to rest in the paradise of God, until my spirit and body shall again reunite, and I am brought forth triumphant through the

air, to meet you before the pleasing bar of the great
Jehovah, the Eternal Judge of both quick and dead.
Amen."[21]

Surely those of us who live in the last days cannot expect to be immune from the sufferings and feelings that
war produces. We hope, however, that we can resist the
coarsening effects of war and its tendency to rob us of any
progress made in developing mercy, meekness, justice,
and so forth.

When we pause to think of nuclear denouement, we
find it almost instantly unthinkable. Yet we know that it is
avoidable *if* mankind will keep God's commandments. If
we do not, then again, as God told us (long before man so
worried about incinerating the world), the earth can be destroyed by fire. The outcome turns on whether mankind
chooses to respond as in Nineveh or as in Sodom, for those
are now the choices; Eden is long since behind us!

Like war, poverty, too, can erode gospel gladness. But
surely we do not presume to lecture the Lord on poverty
either. He has said in connection with His high law of consecration, "But it is not given that one man should possess
that which is above another, wherefore the world lieth in
sin."[22]

The Lord's cure for poverty is the only real cure available, but to be completely effective, it must be done in His
own way. The world's way is the equivalent of using Band-
Aids for arthritis. Of this world's resources, the Lord has
said, "There is enough and to spare."[23] The scarcity lies not
in material resources, but in the love of men toward their
fellowmen and in our lack of justice and mercy.

The people of the city of Enoch knew the sweetness of
shared bread. And, for a few decades, so did the Nephites.
The Lord takes no pleasure in poverty. Yet, without devo-

tion to Him and His commandments, there will be poverty. Jesus foresaw how persistent poverty would be, and how long the poor would be with us.[24]

To what degree we were permitted, before coming here, to see all the outcomes and the risks of mortality, such as war and poverty, we presently know not. A *just* God surely would have let us understand sufficiently about that upon which we are soon to embark. However, with whatever measure of understanding we then had, some "shouted for joy,"[25] a stirring reaction that ought to tell us enough in terms of our perceptions then, when we had some added perspective.

For now, it remains for us to be of good cheer in the midst of all these things that, if properly responded to, can be for our good.

Our human tendency is to forget the Lord, so adversity and afflictions are sometimes needed to put us in remembrance of Him. This should tell us how powerful and consuming the cares and pleasures of the world can become! And, also, how vital it is for us not to misread the role of affliction.[26]

Alma observed how the very poverty of one group of people actually had humbled them so that "they were in a preparation to hear the word."[27] Paradoxically, we pray for peace, but in conditions of peace, some are so slow "to feel after" the Lord that the Lord's counsel is paid little heed.[28]

He who has called us His friends will not fail to tutor us as needed, whatever the conditions. All the more essential it is for us to be of good cheer. How essential it is for us, therefore, to understand first how all the basic justifications for joy are firmly in place.

Certain other teachings of Christ, however, contain within them developmental truths that we might prefer not to face at all. Such truths do not lend themselves to superficial cheeriness. In fact, when these doctrines or teachings first arrive within the circumference of our contemplation, they appear to have a bleakness and austerity about them. We are, nevertheless, expected to have enough faith and determination to explore them—to see what lies below their seemingly icy exterior. If, for instance, the doctrines that have to do with our tutorial training seem wintry or bleak, it remains for us to come to understand that even these reflect the kindness and mercy of God.

However, we must not mistake the seemingly icy implications for divine disinterest. What we are actually encountering is not His disinterest, but our own unfinished self—set off sharply and painfully against that which we must become. If, in recognition, the soul shivers, it is not from a lack of love from the Lord.

The stern sayings of the Savior, when applied, will bring to us expanded personal perspective, deeper personal progress, and a very much enriched future. There will be an enlargement of our capacity to love and to serve, a capacity that is an unending source of everlasting joy. Ironically, it will be personal compliance with the difficult doctrines that one day will drench us in eternal joy! Meanwhile, we will be greatly aided if we can be of good cheer.

One reason we need such extensive experience with routine and repetition in mortality is to learn that there actually are no such things as "routine" and "repetition." Developed capacity to love will teach us that this is so, as we become true sons and daughters of Him whose course is "one eternal round," but whose perfect love insures against boredom.

How could we expect to be joyous and to receive all that "the Father hath" if we do not strive to become like Him?

And, in fact, can we, on our scale, be like Him without sharing in the "fellowship of his sufferings"?[29] He shares with us His work; does that not suggest the need for our sharing, too, some of the suffering as well as the genuine cheer that He has known? Should not we also learn to distinguish, as did He, between temporary sadness and everlasting sorrow? between joy and mere pleasure? In dark days, therefore, we can make our own contribution to illumination by going about our lives just as He has commanded—"with cheerful hearts and countenances."[30]

If in all of this there is some understandable trembling, the adrenalin of affliction can help to ensure that our pace will be brisk rather than casual. His grace will cover us like a cloak—enough to provide for survival but too thin to keep out all the cold. The seeming cold is there to keep us from drowsiness, and gospel gladness warms us enough to keep us going.

So when we say "He lives," we are also asserting how glorious are those realities that are justified cause for being of good cheer. Exploring what He is like (as well as knowing that He lives) provides for us the basic sources of joy and the real causes for cheerfulness. Since we are enjoined to strive to be like Him—disciple, dullard, and rebel alike—it is a breathtaking journey, a journey that can scarcely sustain unless first we learn to be of good cheer.

Footnotes

[1]Matthew 9:2; John 16:33.
[2]3 Nephi 17:20.
[3]John 16:33.
[4]Matthew 9:2.
[5]3 Nephi 1:13.
[6]Acts 23:11.
[7]Acts 27:22.
[8]1 Corinthians 10:13; D&C 50:40.

9D&C 56:11; 64:31.
10Matthew 9:10-13; 6:16.
11Isaiah 53:3-4.
12Philippians 4:4.
13Mosiah 23:28.
14D&C 76:107; 88:106.
15D&C 45:26; 1:35.
16Mormon 8:8; Ether 13:22; 14:21.
17Moroni 1:2.
18D&C 38:29; 45:63; 87:1-2.
19Jacob 6:3; Ether 4:9; D&C 43:32.
20Mormon 8:3, 5.
21Moroni 10:34.
22D&C 49:20.
23D&C 104:17.
24Matthew 26:11.
25Job 38:7.
26Mosiah 23:21.
27Alma 32:6.
28D&C 101:8.
29D&C 84:38; Philippians 3:10.
30D&C 59:15.

6

A Testimony of Jesus Christ

Now, as this volume draws to a close, the author desires to pay personal tribute to and to give further testimony of Jesus Christ, the Son of God.

Usually, when we declare testimony of Him, of necessity we do it in the simplest of terms, emphasizing the glorious reality of His existence, as did Alma: "And Alma went and began to *declare the word* of God unto the church which was established in the valley of Gideon, according to the revelation of the truth of the word which had been spoken by his fathers, and according to the spirit of prophecy which was in him, *according to the testimony of Jesus Christ, the Son of God, who should come to redeem his people from their sins*, and the holy order by which he was called. And thus it is written. Amen."[1]

These dimensions of testifying about Jesus have properly characterized the words of His witnesses in all ages. But as to commandments to be kept and of attributes to be developed, does not Jesus embody and exemplify each and all of these? Should we not, therefore, in testifying of "this

Jesus Christ," also testify of His traits? Should we not also expect that the testimony of Jesus will cause anxiety among the wicked? Some will even "make war" with those who "have the testimony of Jesus Christ."[2]

For John the Beloved,[3] it was not solely the provocativeness of his witness that Jesus Christ lives that stung certain hearers. It was also, for some, the inciting implications—that Christ is a particularized God with a particularized personality, seeking to produce a particularized people—that disturbed.

Today, it is this same ingredient of testimony that causes the resentment and the resistance of many. They reject not only the *actuality* of Jesus but also His *personality* and the attending implications, because His personality carries within it insistent implications for each of us—what we can become and what the standards are by which all mankind will be judged.

If Jesus Christ were merely a name for some sort of vague and nonintervening "life force" in the universe, or if He were someone who had passively given us the Beatitudes but who did not press upon us His way of living, then He might be tolerated, even extolled, by those who otherwise rage against Him and His work. The acceptance of Jesus, however, is the rejection of so much else. Hence those who are too caught up in and entangled with the world cannot bear to be separated from that to which they have given themselves so unreservedly. Some have even grown quite proud of their friendship with the world.

If, therefore, acceptance of the Savior required only occasional genuflection, a periodic calisthenic of conduct, or an affable acknowledgment that He is there, that would be one thing. But to accept His personality as being our own serious model is a wholly different matter. Alas, for some, the latter requires too deep and final disengagement from the things of the secular world upon which so many hearts are so firmly set. As in times past, some mean to keep their place in the synagogue, even if it means losing their place in heaven!

How vastly different, therefore, is fully witnessing to the world that Jesus Christ is "the light, and the life, and the truth of the world."[4]

When we think of Jesus Christ as the Light of the World, not only does His light illuminate the only pathway of life, but His light, in the dusk of civilization's decadence, also reminds us what true light really is.

This book's testimony is gladly given in a time of suffocating secularism with its varied Caesars to whom we are to render. However, no Caesar, even if brilliant or beneficent, can substitute for Christ.

This testimony is likewise given in a time of intense searching for solutions to human problems that, if only by their very massing, proffer an almost unique challenge in history. However, no amount of searching, if it consists of "looking beyond the mark," will produce a true vision of reality. The "mark" is Christ! To look beyond that mark is to fail fatally in perception. And without such perception, there will be no solutions, for without vision, the people perish.

This testimony is also given of Christ in a time when some churches have diluted their commitment to Jesus Christ and to His divinity. Manifestly, no ecclesiastical structure can withstand the world for long without the reinforcing rods of revelation; the resulting erosion will be so rapid that it can be measured in decades, not centuries. The failure of some to acknowledge the divinity of Jesus Christ as *the* Centerpiece of the Christian creed also insures erosion. Unlike the contention of some that Christian religion is odd and irrelevant in a time of strident secularism, the eternal verities tell us just the opposite: That which is not Christocentric is eccentric!

His church and its faithful people strive to follow the counsel of the resurrected Savior, who said, "Therefore, hold up your light that it may shine unto the world. Behold *I am the light which ye shall hold up—that which ye have seen me do.*"[5]

Since some of Jesus' noblest deeds predate His unique Palestinian ministry, we ought to "hold up" that which He did before His mortal ministry—as well as that which He will yet do.

In searching the scriptures that describe God the Father and His Son, Jesus Christ, both as to their *actuality* and their *personality*, one finds that all mortal adjectives, however laudatory, are too anemic. Superlatives are overtaken by ordinariness when applied to them.

In our first estate, Jesus was the incomparable individual among all our Father's spirit children. He helped to prepare this planet for us, and He led—not pushed—us from our premortal post. I thank Him for the untold things He did, across the ages of that first estate (and even earlier), to prepare perfectly for His unique role. I further thank Him, the True Shepherd, for not deserting, then or now, those of us who are slow or stragglers.

I thank Him for encapsulating His exquisite mind in both perfect love and perfect humility. His brilliance is not the "catch-me-if-you-can" kind, but a pleading and patient "Come, follow me."

His premortal performance reflected both an astonishing selflessness and a breathtaking commitment to freedom as a condition of our genuine growth. I thank Him for combining His long view of our needs with that short step forward so long ago to volunteer His service as our Savior. Never has anyone offered so much to so many in so few words as did Jesus when He said, "Here am I, send me."[6]

His duties have long been galactic, yet He noticed the widow casting in her mite. I am stunned at His perfect, unconditional love of all. Indeed, "I stand all amazed at the love Jesus offers me."[7] I thank Him for His discerning way of loving us without controlling us, for never letting the needs of now crowd out the considerations of eternity.

I thank Him, in every situation, for maintaining His grip on Himself, which was also mankind's hold on the eternal future.

He who did not need to die himself was willing to be bound by the chains of death in order that He could break them for all mankind. In eloquent example, He partook voluntarily and submissively of the bitter cup in the awful but, for Him, avoidable Atonement.

He was raised in a lowly town and gave us the example of rising above His beginnings but without renouncing them.

He is the perfect leader. He does not ask us to do what He left undone, nor to endure what He avoided or failed to endure. I thank Him for truly teaching us about our personal possibilities and for giving us directions by example—not merely by pointing.

He gives us enough, but not more than we can manage. I thank Him who did everything perfectly for sharing His precious work with those of us who then do it so imperfectly.

Just as He helped Father to create the universe, He also helped Father to create each of our little universes of needed experience, which can be for our good.

I thank Him for forgoing fashionableness and not only for enduring the absence of deserved appreciation but also for speaking the truth, knowing beforehand that cruel misunderstanding and misrepresentation would follow.

I thank Him for His marvelous management of time, for never misusing a moment; even His seconds showed His stewardship.

No Son ever complemented His Father so gracefully, honored His Father so constantly, or trusted His Father so completely as did Jesus.

Whether He is descriptively designated as Creator, Only Begotten Son, Prince of Peace, Advocate, Mediator, Son of God, Savior, Messiah, Author and Finisher of Salvation, King of kings—I witness that Jesus Christ is the only name under heaven whereby one can be saved.

I testify that He is utterly incomparable in what He *is*, what He *knows*, what He has *accomplished*, and what He has *experienced*. Yet, movingly, He calls us His friends.[8]

We can trust, worship, and even adore Him without any reservation. As the only perfect person to sojourn on this planet, there is none like Him.

In intelligence and performance, He far surpasses the individual and the composite capacities and achievements of all who have lived, live now, and will yet live.

He rejoices in our genuine goodness and achievement, but any assessment of where we stand in relation to Him tells us that we do not stand at all. We kneel.

Can we, even in the depths of disease, tell Him anything at all about suffering? In ways we cannot comprehend, our sicknesses and infirmities were borne by Him even before they were borne by us. The very weight of our combined sins caused Him to descend below all. We have never been, nor will we be, in depths such as He has known. Thus His atonement made perfect His empathy and His mercy and His capacity to succor us, for which we can be everlastingly grateful as He tutors us in our trials. There was no ram in the thicket at Calvary to spare Him, this Friend of Abraham and Isaac.

Can those who yearn for hearth or home instruct Him as to what it is like to be homeless or on the move? Did He not say in a disclosing moment that "the foxes have holes, and the birds of the air have nests; but the Son of man hath not where to lay his head"?[9]

Can we really counsel Him about being misrepresented, misunderstood, or betrayed? Or what it is like when even friends falter or "go a fishing"?[10]

Can we educate Him regarding injustice or compare failures of judicial systems with the Giver of the Law, who knew what perfect justice was, yet in divine dignity endured its substantive and procedural perversion?

And when we feel so alone, can we presume to teach Him who trod "the wine-press alone" anything at all about feeling forsaken?

Cannot the childless who crave children count on His empathy? For He loved children and said, "Of such is the kingdom of heaven." "He wept, and . . . one by one, [He] blessed them, and prayed unto the Father for them. And when he had done this he wept again."[11]

Do we presume to instruct Him in either compassion or mercy? Even at the apogee of His agony upon the cross, He, in selfless love, consoled a thief beside Him, saying, "To day shalt thou be with me in paradise."[12]

Can we excuse our compromises because of the powerful temptations of status seeking? It was He who displayed incredible integrity as the adversary made Him an offer that could not be refused—"all the kingdoms of the world, and the glory of them."[13] But He refused!

Can we teach Him about meekness while enduring

irony? His remaining possession, a cloak, was gambled for even as He died. Yet the very earth was His footstool! Jesus gave mankind living water so that we shall never thirst again, yet on the cross He was given vinegar.

Can we lecture Him on liberty, He who sets us free from our last enemies—sin and death?

Can those who revere human freedom yet complain about human suffering ever achieve real reconciliation except through His gospel?

Can those concerned with nourishing the poor advise Him concerning feeding the multitudes?

Can those who are concerned with medicine instruct Him about healing the sick?

Or can we inform the Atoner about feeling the sting of ingratitude when one's service goes unappreciated or unnoticed? Only one leper in ten thanked Jesus, who asked searchingly, "But where are the nine?"[14]

Should those concerned with lengthening the lifespan offer to enlighten the Resurrector of all mankind?

Can scientists, whose discipline brings the discovery of the interweavings in the tapestry of truth, instruct the Tapestry Maker?

Should we seek to counsel Him in courage? Should we rush forth eagerly to show Him our press clippings and mortal medals—our scratches and bruises—as He bears His five special wounds?

Does not the "word of [His] power" actually bring entire new worlds into being and cause others to pass away? Yet in the midst of such galactic governance, He interviewed His Twelve unhurriedly "one by one,"[15] and later called a farm boy in rural New York.

Has He not invited us to observe His cosmic craftsmanship in the heavens that we might see "God moving in his majesty and power"?[16] But do we not also see Him moving in His majesty and power as each prodigal finally completes his homeward orbit?

Though His creations are so vast as to be numberless even to computerized man, has Jesus not told us that the very hairs of our head are numbered?[17]

Did not the resurrected Jesus stand by an imprisoned Paul, telling him to "be of good cheer" and calling him on his mission to Rome?[18] Likewise, Jesus stands by the righteous in all their individual ordeals.

Did not this good and true Shepherd forgo repose after the glorious but awful Atonement in order to establish His work among the lost sheep who were disobedient in the days of Noah? Did He not then visit still other lost sheep in the Americas? Then still other lost sheep?[19] What can we tell Him about conscientiousness?

Indeed, we cannot teach Him anything! But we can listen to Him. We can love Him; we can honor Him; we can worship Him. We can keep His commandments, and we can feast upon His scriptures.

Yes, we who are so forgetful and even rebellious are never forgotten by Him. We *are* His "work" and His "glory," and He is *never* distracted. We are the "people of His pasture and sheep of His hand."[20]

Therefore, in addition to my boundless admiration of His achievements and my adoration of Him for what He is—knowing that my superlatives are too shallow to do more than echo his excellence—as one of Jesus' special witnesses in the fulness of times, I attest to the fulness of His ministry.

How dare some treat His ministry as if it were all beatitudes and no declaratives! How myopic it is to view His ministry as all crucifixion and no resurrection! How provincial to perceive it as all Calvary and no Palmyra; all rejection at a village called Capernaum and no acceptance in the City of Enoch; all relapse and regression in ancient Israel and no Bountiful with its ensuing decades of righteousness!

Jesus Christ is the Jehovah of the Red Sea and of Sinai, the Resurrected Lord, the spokesman for the Father in the theophany at Palmyra—a Palmyra pageant with a precious audience of one!

He lives today, mercifully granting unto all nations as much light as they can bear and messengers of their own to teach them. And who better than the Light of the world can decide the degree of divine disclosure—whether it is to be flashlights or floodlights?

Soon, however, all flesh shall see Him together. All knees shall bow in His presence, and all tongues confess His name.[21] Knees that never before have assumed *that* posture for *that* purpose will do so then—and promptly. Tongues that never before have spoken His name except in gross profanity will do so then—and worshipfully.

Soon, He who was once mockingly dressed in purple will come again, attired in red apparel, reminding us whose blood redeemed us.[22] All will then acknowledge the completeness of His justice and His mercy and will see how human indifference to God—not God's indifference to humanity—accounts for so much misery and suffering. Then we will see the true story of mankind—and not through glass darkly. The great military battles will appear as mere bonfires that blazed briefly, and the mortal accounts of the human experience will be but graffiti on the walls of time.

Before that reckoning moment, however, both your ministry and mine will unfold in the grim but also glorious circumstances of the last days.

Yes, there will be wrenching polarization on this planet, but also the remarkable reunion with our colleagues in Christ from the city of Enoch. Yes, nation after nation will become a house divided, but more and more unifying Houses of the Lord will grace this planet. Yes, Armageddon lies ahead—but so does Adam-ondi-Ahman!

Meanwhile, did not Jesus tell us what to expect by way of heat in the final summer? Did He not also say that He would prove our faith and our patience by trial?

Did He not provide a needed sense of proportion when He spoke of the comparative few who will find the narrow way leading to the strait gate? Did He not also say that His Saints, scattered upon all the face of the earth, would, in the midst of wickedness, commotion, and persecution, be "armed with righteousness and with the power of God," for He is determined to have "a pure people"?[23]

His work proceeds forward almost as if in the comparative calmness of the eye of a storm. First, He reigns in the midst of His saints; soon, in all the world.

So as the shutters of human history begin to close as if before a gathering storm, and as events scurry across the human scene like so many leaves before a wild wind, those who stand before the warm glow of the gospel fire can be permitted a shiver of the soul. Yet in our circle of certitude we know, even in the midst of all these things, that there will be no final frustration of God's purposes. God has known "all things from the beginning; wherefore, he prepareth a way to accomplish all his works among the children of men."[24]

Thus, gladly and unashamedly, I add my small voice to the anthem of apostolic appreciation by acknowledging and adoring Jesus of Nazareth, Savior and King.

I witness that *He lives*—with all that those simple words imply—knowing that I will be held accountable for this testimony; but, as readers, you are now accountable for my witness, which I give in love and sobriety, but most importantly, in the very and holy name of Jesus Christ! Amen.

Footnotes

[1]Alma 6:8. Italics added.
[2]Revelation 12:17.
[3]See Revelation 1:1-7.
[4]Ether 4:12.
[5]3 Nephi 18:24. Italics added.
[6]Abraham 3:27.
[7]*Hymns*, no. 80.
[8]John 15:15.
[9]Matthew 8:20.
[10]John 21:3.
[11]Matthew 19:14; 3 Nephi 17:21-22.
[12]Luke 23:43.
[13]Matthew 4:8.
[14]Luke 17:17.
[15]Moses 1:35; 3 Nephi 28:1.
[16]D&C 88:47.
[17]Matthew 10:30; Moses 1:38.
[18]Acts 23:11.
[19]1 Peter 3:18-20; John 10:16; 3 Nephi 15:17, 21; 16:1-3.
[20]Moses 1:39; Psalm 95:7.
[21]D&C 76:110-11; Philippians 2:10-11.
[22]D&C 133:48-49.
[23]1 Nephi 14:12-14; D&C 100:16.
[24]1 Nephi 9:6.

Index